SAFE AS HOUSES

Gerard Lemos has been a social housing consultant and trainer on race and equal opportunities since 1989. He has worked for both housing associations and local authorities as well as the Housing Corporation. He is the author of *Interviewing Perpetrators of Racial Harassment*, published by Lemos & Crane.

The author gratefully acknowledges the Chartered Institute of Housing and Circle 33 Housing Trust for the use of extracts from their previously published materials. Thanks are also due to Charlie Forman for his suggestions and additions to this book.

SAFE AS HOUSES

A GUIDE TO SUPPORTING PEOPLE EXPERIENCING RACIAL HARASSMENT IN HOUSING

Gerard Lemos

First published in Great Britain 1997

Lemos & Crane
20 Pond Square, Highgate
London N6 6BA

© Lemos & Crane 1997

ISBN: 1-898001-33-2

A CIP catalogue record for this book is available from the British Library.

Cover, text design and setting by
Mick Keates/Concise Artisans, London

Printed by Redwood Books, Trowbridge

CONTENTS

INTRODUCTION

What is covered in the book? / Who is the
book for? / Existing policies and procedures /
*The Tenants' Guarantee / Chartered Institute
of Housing Management Standards /*
Policies for the future

This book on supporting those experiencing racial
harassment is a companion volume to *Eliminating Racial
Harassment – a guide to housing policies and procedures* and
*Interviewing Perpetrators of Racial Harassment – a guide for
housing managers.* The current book also sits alongside a
book in Arden's Housing Library, *Nuisance and
Harassment – Law and practice in the management of social
housing.* These four books published by Lemos & Crane
taken together should provide housing managers with the
most comprehensive good practice guidance available on
dealing with racial harassment. Alongside these, the
National Directory of Action Against Racial Harassment
details practice in some 200 statutory and voluntary organisations nation-wide.

The two inquiries that have been conducted by the

Home Affairs Select Committee and the Racial Attacks Group's report[1] were the first widely accepted official acknowledgements of the problem of racial harassment. They have all endorsed a multi-agency approach to dealing effectively with racial harassment. It has, however, been harder to turn it into a reality on the ground. The problems with the multi-agency approach are discussed in the book, with a view to developing ways of making it a practical reality, particularly in support for people experiencing harassment.

It is arguable at a casework level that the multi-agency approach has been least effective. This book provides practical guidance on how it can be made to work effectively across disciplines, organisations and vested interests. In this approach, individual agencies with limited powers are not left in isolation to deal with this major social problem, which does not fit into neat bureaucratic definitions and structures.

The book is also designed to offer good practice guidance on handling cases and how to support those experiencing racial harassment, showing

- what it is reasonable for them to expect
- the extent to which social landlords and others can fulfil those expectations
- ways of ensuring that incidents are reported and how to conduct interviews effectively
- practical support that can be offered thereafter.

---

[1]There has been a series of reports published both by the Home Office (1981, 1989, 1991) and the Home Affairs Select Committee (1986, 1988).

What is covered in the book?

The book starts by setting the context and giving an overview of both the problem and suggested approaches to its resolution. Part I deals with the multi-agency approach to supporting people experiencing racial harassment.

Part II deals with best practice in supporting people experiencing harassment. Chapter 4 lists their expectations. Chapter 5 is about ensuring that racial incidents are reported.

Chapter 6 is a detailed analysis of the interviewing skills needed for supporting those experiencing racial harassment. Chapter 7 gives comprehensive guidance on conducting the first interview of the person who has been attacked after an incident has been reported.

Chapter 8 discusses the various forms of practical support that can be offered and Chapter 9 deals with follow-up visits.

Throughout the book there are case studies of good practice drawn from social housing and community organisations.

Who is the book for?

The book is designed principally to help housing managers fulfil the landlord function in social housing such that tenants of all ethnic backgrounds can live peacefully in their own homes. Racial harassment does not of course occur only in housing. It is part of a wider social problem of racial attacks on the street and in schools, for example. The book therefore also gives information and practical suggestions to other agencies such as the police, education authorities, social services and environmental health departments of local authorities, community organisations and solicitors.

The book is also aimed at practitioners. Many people do not deal with cases of racial harassment all the time, and so may not have a body of experience and expertise to draw on when cases arise. Suggested approaches are offered which will also be helpful to those new to dealing with cases of racial harassment. Managers will also find it useful in supervising staff who are dealing with cases. Lastly, policy makers will be able to draw from it in devising new policies and reviewing existing ones.

Existing policies and procedures

The need for social landlords, as for other agencies such as the police, schools and education authorities, to have clear and effective policies is now well-documented. They ensure that staff understand their responsibilities, that people who are harassed know what they can expect in the way of support, and that actual or potential perpetrators know what the consequences might be for them.

Policies and procedures for social landlords are discussed at length in *Eliminating Racial Harassment – Policies and procedures for dealing with racial harassment*. It is not intended to repeat that guidance here. Standards of best practice identified by lead bodies, such as the Department of the Environment, the Housing Corporation and the Chartered Institute of Housing, are given below. The guidance given by the Commission for Racial Equality is covered in some detail in *Eliminating Racial Harassment*. In addition, the direction that policies will need to take in the future is also set out below.

The Tenants' Guarantee

The Housing Corporation in its 'Performance Standards for Housing Associations' requires housing associations to have a policy framework within which to deal with harassment:

> 'Associations must endeavour to deal with harassment of or by their tenants. In particular they must have policies and procedures to assist tenants who are suffering from harassment and nuisance.'[2]

This recognition of the need for effective policies and procedures is reflected in Department of the Environment research (*Racial Incidents in Council Housing: The Local Authority Response*).[3] This indicates that many local authorities in multi-racial areas have in the last few years adopted policies and procedures for racial harassment. Of the 85 local authorities who returned detailed questionnaires to the survey, over half had a policy before 1989, and one-

[2]Housing Corporation guidance to the registered social landlords they regulate is frequently updated. An expectation that they deal effectively with harassment is a persistent feature. *The Tenants' Guarantee* (1994) gives statutory force to some of these requirements, including those on harassment.
[3]Department of the Environment, 1994, HMSO.

fifth had adopted a policy since then. As many again were considering adopting a policy. Only six per cent had no plans for a policy.

The most definitive statement on an effective strategy has been identified in this research by Brunel University. They outline some of the key components:

Objectives and organisation
- Commitment by elected members and top managers is essential

Policy
- Responsibilities of officers must be precisely defined
- Information from many sources must be pooled
- Aims must be clearly stated and widely disseminated
- Resources can be found given the will

Putting policy into practice
- Formulate an action plan for putting policy into practice
- Allocate officer responsibility for implementing policy
- Introduce appropriate training

Prevention
- Monitor danger areas and improve estate security and environment
- Community development measures can contribute
- Anticipate problems and avoid putting people at risk

Support to victims
- Record all incidents fully and report them quickly
- Interview victims for the full facts, providing interpreters if necessary

- Maintain and support victims on estates whenever possible, transfer victims whenever this is necessary

Dealing with perpetrators
- Evidence must be gathered quickly and recorded fully and appropriately
- Management action can be effective
- Legal advice should be sought and appropriate action taken

Monitoring and review
- Monitoring must be simple, adaptable and co-ordinated with other agencies
- Reporting of information gathered should be regular
- Review of policy effectiveness is required every two to four years[4]

Chartered Institute of Housing Management Standards

The Chartered Institute of Housing recommends the following standards[5] for supporting people experiencing racial or sexual harassment:

Have time targets for promptly responding to and investigating all reported incidents of harassment.

Carry out investigations in a sensitive, victim orientated manner.

[4] Department of the Environment (1994), HMSO.
[5] The Chartered Institute of Housing, *Housing Management Standards*.

Give victims the option of being interviewed by a person of the same sex or ethnic group, wherever possible.

Interview victims at their home wherever possible and ensure that any office interviews are conducted in privacy.

Provide customers with advice and information about the various remedies for harassment and about agencies in addition to the landlord, which provide assistance and support in dealing with the problem.

Refer victims to specialist counselling and support agencies such as victim support groups, harassment support groups and women's centres as appropriate.

Interview alleged perpetrators only with the consent of the complainant.

Report incidents of racial and sexual harassment to the police provided the victim consents.

Where racial harassment is a particular problem, provide or work with other agencies jointly to provide a 24-hour telephone line or alarm system so that vitims can immediately report incidents and summon help.

Provide or lend emergency alarm systems to victims at risk of further harassment to enable them to call for assistance quickly.

Ensure that the homes of tenants who are victims of racial or sexual harassment have appropriate security precautions, for example, adequate window and door locks and safety letter boxes which extinguish burning material.

Treat as emergencies 'make safe' repairs to the homes of victims of harassment.

Ensure that sexist, racist, homophobic and obscene graffiti is removed within 24 hours of it coming to the landlord's attention.

> Arrange for tenant victims who are at risk of violence to be temporarily or permanently rehoused if this is what they want.

Policies for the future

There is a well-established and widely accepted need for clear, effective policies which are 'victim-centred'. Despite this, where landlords are aware of cases of persistent racial harassment it is far more common to find the people experiencing harassment being forced to move rather than to see the perpetrators evicted or effectively restrained by injunctions, although the number of successful actions is rising.[6] The good intentions of policies have not always been easy to translate into action. The result has been that one of the principal tenets of that policy approach has largely failed – that perpetrators of harassment should be evicted, and the people being attacked can continue to live in their homes in peace.

There is clearly therefore a need for a review that focuses not specifically on taking action against perpetrators, or punishing people for racist behaviour, but primarily concentrates on what is in the best interests of the person being harassed as they define it. This will invariably mean that the unacceptable behaviour – the attacks on people or

---

[6]In 1993 social landlords served 130 notices of seeking possession. 10 households were evicted. Figures are from *Racial Attacks and Harassment: the Response of Social Landlords*, Department of the Environment 1996.

property – should stop. People being harassed are often not keen to pursue action against perpetrators. First they fear reprisals against themselves and secondly they do not particularly wish to seek revenge or have vindictive motives. They are much more concerned generally for the safety and security of themselves and their families.

PART I

CONTEXT AND OVERVIEW

CHAPTER 1

RACIAL HARASSMENT IN BRITAIN TODAY

A long-standing problem / The current situation / Who is involved? / Harassment is an abuse of power / The impact on people experiencing harassment / Deaths resulting from racial harassment / Where does racial harassment take place? / Harassment in particular circumstances / *Neighbourhoods of multiple deprivation / Organised far right activity* / Racial harassment and different tenures / Common misconceptions about racial harassment / *The way ahead*

A long-standing problem

On 10 June 1919 in Bute Town, Cardiff, a black seaman was killed and many others injured when a group of some 2,500 white men went on the rampage. The following day *The Times* described the situation in Liverpool, another port with a long-standing and substantial black population, in this way:

'The police have issued a warning that severe measures will be taken against anyone attempting to wreck property or to attack members of the coloured community, many of whom are inoffensive and have given distinguished service during the war. Scores of coloured men and women, some of them with their families, have gone to the local police headquarters asking for protection, and last evening over 60 of them were taken into the care of the police.'[7]

Evidently racial harassment is hardly a new phenomenon. For many years, however, attempts to draw attention to the situation were greeted with official denials from, for example, the police, the Home Office and local authorities. It was not so much that attacks were taking place that was denied, but the racist motive. Acknowledging that motive provides an insight into the fear and intimidation the person on whom the attack is perpetrated might feel.

The denials took two forms, both in their way perfidious, if not deliberate, delusions. The first was that these incidents were not targeted, deliberate attacks but just inter-racial conflicts, borne of mutual intolerance, for which both parties were equally responsible.

As attacks were invariably perpetrated by white people on black people,[8] who equally invariably did not retaliate, this theory owes much to the need to reassure the authorities' complacency and inertia, and owes nothing to the need to support those who have been attacked.

---

[7] Peter Fryer's magnificent survey, *Staying Power – the history of black people in Britain*, 1984 Pluto Press, contains this and many other early examples of racial attacks.
[8] See page 18 below.

This theory of inter-racial conflict persisted amongst police forces. The consequence of this myth is that all incidents in which members of different races were involved, regardless of motives, initiators or outcomes, were classified together. As a result, those incidents that were in fact harassment were not dealt with from the perspective of supporting those who had been attacked, but instead, in some cases, led to the victims being blamed for the attacks.

The other enduring myth is that racial attacks were 'just kids' or 'vandalism', or 'anti-social behaviour', and could therefore be dealt with by 'a quiet word' or 'a ticking off', or some such inconsequential and minimal action. This archaic notion from some probably non-existent past is complacency mathematically squared, once for inaction, then for seeking to justify the inaction.

From the early incidents described above throughout the period of post-1945 migrations from the Caribbean and the Indian sub-continent, allegations of violence and attacks by both members of the police and the public persisted.

Robert Miles in his article 'Racism and Fascism in Contemporary Europe'[9] comments:

> 'The allegations were officially and persistently denied. Yet, activists within these communities persevered in exposing the racist violence that they and members of their community experienced. During the late 1970s a campaign against violence gathered impetus in many English cities, bringing together immediate victims,

[9] *New Community* July 1994.

political activists within the communities of the victims and "official" politicians (especially from the Labour Party). By the early 1980s, the campaign had gained sufficient political support and had assembled sufficient evidence to persuade one of the central institutions of the British State, the Home Office, to undertake its own survey of the extent of racist violence in Britain (1981)... Statistical representations of the incidents of racial violence may demonstrate not only an increase in the number of such incidents, but also an increase in the willingness to report such incidents. Both could be true at the same time.'

The current situation

No one knows the extent, seriousness and frequency of racial attacks in this country. What is known is that there is serious under-reporting and under-recording. There is, however, now widespread agreement, at least insofar as the contemporary situation is concerned, that there is a significant problem and, apart from a small diminution in reported cases in the Metropolitan Police area[10] in the early 1990s, a problem that appears in many areas to be increasing and is certainly not evidentially decreasing.

The most recent statistics for reported incidents in 1994 have once more shown an increase of 20 per cent in reported racially motivated incidents. In the year between April 1993 and March 1994, 9,762 racial incidents were

[10] Statistics collected by the Home Office for police forces in England and Wales.

recorded by police forces in England and Wales. By far the highest number (3,889) was in the Metropolitan Police area. Thus the need for intervention by the authorities and community groups both to prevent and solve the problem is as compelling as it has ever been.

The Home Office and the police accept that racial attacks are not always reported. In the past separate records of racially motivated incidents were not kept, particularly by the police. More recently the police have set up a separate record-keeping system, although for the reasons already given inter-racial incidents have sometimes been confusingly recorded alongside racial harassment and attacks. The question should not be 'Were the protagonists of different races?' but 'Was one targeting the other because of their race?'.

So exact numbers of racial incidents – name-calling, verbal abuse, attacks on property, theft and physical attacks on the person motivated by race or skin colour – are hard to come by. Many are not reported, and others which are do not get recorded as being racially motivated. The British Crime Survey, which provides the most authoritative assessment, estimated in 1993 a total of 130,000 such incidents per year.[11] Only 7,793 were reported to the police and recorded as such, although others may have been reported to other agencies, including landlords. Other surveys, such as the one done by Home Office researchers in North Plaistow (see page 49), suggest that reports to the police and other authorities under-estimate the number of incidents by a factor as high as 30.[12]

[11]British Crime Survey, HMSO.
[12]Saulsbury W and Bowling B (1991), *The Multi-agency Approach in Practice*, The North Plaistow Racial Harassment Project, Home Office.

Many researchers and practitioners believe that not only the number of reported incidents is rising but so is the total number of incidents. They consider that this is not confined to the United Kingdom, but is a Europe-wide phenomenon which may also be linked to the rise of far right activity since 1989.[13]

By far the clearest indication of under-reporting is given whenever social landlords survey their tenants to establish how many have been the targets of racial attacks or harassment.

A housing association with a large stock in the London Borough of Tower Hamlets received two complaints of racial harassment from an estate on which it had many Asian tenants, most of whom had only recently moved in. Nearby parts of the borough are notorious for racial attacks and in the Isle of Dogs a British National Party representative was elected briefly to the Council in 1994.

The association surveyed all the tenants on the estate and found that, despite receiving only two reports of harassment, all 26 Asian families living there had at various times been the target of racial attacks.

Who is involved?

The people who are harassed in this way are predominantly black or from an ethnic minority. Research from all

---

[13] For a European perspective, see *The Ford Report* (1991) European Parliament. Its full title is *Report drawn up on behalf of the Committee of Inquiry on Racism and Xenophobia on the findings of the Committee of Inquiry*, Luxembourg: OOPEC.

around the country including Leeds, Birmingham, Leicester, Nottingham and London[14] indicates that people from the Indian sub-continent are the most likely targets, but all members of racial groups who are visibly different, usually because of skin colour, are at higher risk than white people. Women and older people are at a significantly greater risk of harassment, rather suggesting that the perpetrators are cowards as well as harassers.

The people who harass them are white, usually young and male. This was established by the Policy Studies Institute in the research that took place in the writing of *Black and White Britain* in 1984: 'the typical perpetrator is a white teenager, often part of a gang and sometimes encouraged by parents.'[15] Nothing that has happened since suggests that this situation has changed, and although many incidents do not fit this pattern the majority do. These findings are confirmed in more recent research, for example in North Plaistow,[16] and indeed in the police's own statistics.

Harassment is an abuse of power

Harassment is neither mutual intolerance nor anti-social behaviour. It is a targeted, deliberate, continuing abuse of

[14] Many local authority committee reports on racial harassment have been collected and made available through the Local Authority Race Relations Information Exchange (LARRIE).

[15] Brown C (1984), *Black and White Britain*, Policy Studies Institute.

[16] Saulsbury W and Bowling B (1991), *The Multi-agency Approach in Practice*, The North Plaistow Racial Harassment Project, Home Office.

power by those who think themselves stronger or superior against those held to be weaker and inferior. This power and ideology of superiority is undoubtedly founded on prejudice, but may in practical terms be manifested only in superior numbers – a gang of youths taking on an unsuspecting individual. Power taken and abused is, in playground phraseology, not picking on someone your own size.

It follows that race is not the only reason why people are attacked or harassed. Apart from race, people are attacked without cause or justification and in a way designed to intimidate because of their sex, their age or disability, because they are lesbians or gay men, among other reasons.

The impact on people experiencing harassment

A report by Manchester Council for Community Relations in 1986 stressed that one should

> 'remember the reality which lies behind all of these cases – an individual or family living in fear, subject to humiliation, stress and physical danger, frequently too terrified for their safety to allow children to play outside, driven to tranquillisers and sleeping pills, constantly on the alert wondering if tonight will bring a brick through the window, or tomorrow morning the letters "NF – pakis go home" on their front door.'[17]

---

[17] Quoted in Lemos G (1993), *Interviewing Perpetrators of Racial Harassment*, Lemos & Crane.

A Birmingham City Council survey, *The Support Needs of Tenants Suffering Racial Harassment*, draws some interesting conclusions on the impact of racial incidents on the life and emotions of those who experience it. It comments, for example, that 'racial harassment has a devastating effect on a person's psychological and emotional state'.

Disturbingly, researchers had to suspend some of the interviews with those who have experienced harassment when they asked about the emotional impact as respondents became very upset. Other respondents commented, 'Sometimes I feel like I am going mad', 'I am depressed, on tablets. Too frightened to go out', 'I get worked up, I cry. I am frightened to be on my own in the evening'.

The impact of the psychological effect on the routines of daily life were also disturbing in this survey. Some examples were: 'I cannot sleep at night. I keep all the lights on'; 'go and visit daughter most of the time'; 'stop children from playing out...they should be outside...not stuck in...they get on top of me because they want to play out'; 'the youngest has nightmares'; 'afraid to go out...prisoner in my own house...'; 'nerves constantly on edge...it has affected the way I treat the children. I shout at them a lot. I know it is not their fault'.[18]

Apart from the emotional and physical harm that attacks cause, they can also result in people either temporarily or permanently having to leave their home.

---

[18]Birmingham City Council Housing Department (1993), *The Support Needs of Tenants Suffering Racial Harassment – findings and recommendations of a research survey.*

Deaths resulting from racial harassment

In the worst cases, people have been killed in their own home, for example by arson, like Mohammed Younis Khan in Newham, East London.[19] There have also been well-documented cases of racial killings on the street, such as the murder of Stephen Lawrence in Greenwich in 1993 while standing at a bus stop, by white youths hurling racial abuse. In November 1994 an Asian shopkeeper, Mohan Singh Kullar, was left for dead after an attack in an alley behind his shop in Cimla, a predominantly white suburb of Neath in South Wales with no known history of racial animosity, at least to white people. He died a few days later in hospital.[20]

The Runnymede Trust estimated that between 1970 and 1989, 74 people died as a result of attacks believed to be racially motivated.[21]

Where does racial harassment take place?

People are harassed on the street, in their shops, in schools and in their homes. Harassment in the home is perhaps the most disturbing and undermining because for most people, home, apart from representing physical shelter, also stands for security, warmth and comfort. In this context, an attack to or in the home is experienced as

[19] This incident is powerfully described in a BBC Tuesday Documentary, *Black* (1984).
[20] See *The Guardian*, several reports in November 1994.
[21] Skellington and Morris (1992), *Race in Britain Today*, Sage.

a fundamental emotional violation.

The inner cities are best known for a high incidence of racially motivated attacks. The combination of economic disadvantage and high unemployment, a poor physical environment, a history of multi-racial tension and proportionally larger concentrations of black and minority ethnic people may produce a relatively higher incidence. It is worth remembering, however, that racial attacks can occur where black and minority ethnic people are isolated in areas with, by comparison, a less high profile of inter-racial tension.

Of the 5 million black and ethnic minority people in Britain, 200,000 identified themselves to the 1991 census as living in rural areas, but rarely in large groups or communities. The Runnymede Trust documented cases of harassment in Shrewsbury and Finchley.[22] *The Guardian* commented on the fatal attack on Mohan Singh Kullar, the Asian shopkeeper in Neath: 'the assault has raised an uncomfortable spectre for Wales, which has prided itself on being free of racial violence prevalent in the rest of Britain'.[23]

A report, *Not in Norfolk – tackling the invisibility of racism*, produced by Norfolk and Norwich Racial Equality Council in 1994, chronicled harassment that can arise in rural areas. A mother described a visit to picturesque Wells-next-the-Sea with her children:

[22] Gordon P (1986), *Racial Violence and Harassment*, Runnymede Trust.
[23] *The Guardian*, November 1994.

'We noticed a gang of half a dozen or so youths ahead of us. As soon as they caught sight of us, they leapt in the air shouting "Sieg Heil, Sieg Heil!" and giving their Nazi salute. They'd spotted one of my girls, a 15-year-old of African descent. She was the only non-white child visible. They began yelling "Nigger girl out, nigger girl out". Then they began following us, still yelling after us. There were plenty of people around, all white, all carefully looking in the other direction. I saw a police car heading towards us. I flagged it down, told the PC inside what had happened, and asked him if he'd make a formal report and let the gang know I had reported the incident. The PC said there was nothing he could do about it; he knew who was in that gang and the way they behaved and I should hear the things they called him.'[24]

Apparently many people in Norfolk think there is 'no problem here'. On the contrary, the problem seems to be little different to elsewhere. There are, of course, many black people living in Norfolk who have not been harassed, but nonetheless, 'the places where black people reported encountering overt harassment most commonly and directly, were schools, workplace, housing estates and pubs, clubs and take-aways'.

At the end of 1995 the leader of the Liberal Democrats, Paddy Ashdown, whilst out with a local clergyman in his constituency in seemingly peaceful and largely white Yeovil investigating a recent spate of attacks against Indian restaurateurs, was threatened with a knife. The local newspaper

[24]Derbyshire H (1994), *Not in Norfolk – tackling the invisibility of racism*, Norfolk and Norwich Racial Equality Council.

that initially reported the attacks had already suffered an arson attack on their offices after carrying the reports.[25]

Mr Ashdown has been so concerned about the attacks that he was instrumental in establishing a new organisation, 'Partners against Racial Harassment'.

Harassment in particular circumstances

Neighbourhoods of multiple deprivation

Some housing estates have now become areas of multiple deprivation. Unemployment is high. Crime, often by juveniles, particularly car theft and burglary, is widespread. Problems of disrepair are endemic. It would be quite wrong to regard such estates as being beyond help. Indeed there are many examples of investment, revitalisation and community development leading to the transformation of such areas into places where people want to go to live, not places from which people want to escape.

Before such transformations occur, however, these multiple problems can seem intractable with the result that when problems of nuisance or harassment occur, the first response of the person being harassed is that they want a transfer. Indeed, in many cases they wanted to move before the incident of harassment, but this may be the final straw, or they may be sufficiently familiar with the landlord's policies to know that because of their commitment to dealing effectively with harassment, this is one of the few remaining ways to get a transfer.

[25] These incidents were widely reported in *The Guardian* and *The Independent*.

In this context of widespread deprivation and dissatis-
faction, it is far more difficult to support people experiencing harassment in their own homes. Much of the guidance given in this book is based on the assumption, which
is more often the case than not, that people are moderate-
ly content with their current home, and would not, were it
not for the harassment, even consider the possibility of
moving. Nonetheless there is a need also to deal with the
fact that people's wish to move may indeed be precipitat-
ed by harassment, but may also be part of a longer history
which needs to be considered both in trying to stop the
harassment and in responding to the request for a transfer.

Organised far right activity

Some incidents and campaigns of harassment are politi-
cally motivated and organised by far right groups. In these
circumstances, the perpetrators will often 'hunt in packs'
and attack where they are not known or recognised. They
may therefore not be tenants of the same landlord as the
person being harassed. They may also not be known to
local witnesses. So it is difficult for housing managers to
have much impact in preventing the harassment, or in
seeking to make the perpetrators desist.

These circumstances will inevitably require responses
from the police either in banning such demonstrations
where they have been trailed in advance, or in acting quickly to identify and prosecute perpetrators. The new offence
of intentional harassment created in the Criminal Justice
and Public Order Act 1995 will, it is hoped, assist here.

In addition collective action through demonstrations

and, in extreme circumstances, protection from vigilante groups have also had an impact, for example in London's East End. It is a sad and worrying commentary on the authorities' ability and willingness to deal with this problem, that people have felt the need to organise to protect themselves. This response is nonetheless understandable, indeed predictable. In some areas it may even be the only effective one, but its dangers are underlined by the death of a white youth, Richard Everitt, in Somers Town north London in 1994.[26]

Racial harassment and different tenures

Much of the debate about racial attacks and harassment focuses on local authority estates. It is of course not the case that attacks are confined to council tenants or to people who live on estates. In some cases described above people were attacked in shops. Incidents also occur in schools, and many education authorities have developed policies and procedures for dealing with bullying and harassment. The education authorities' response is discussed in greater detail in chapter 2.

Owner occupiers can also be the target for attacks. In some instances the person being attacked or harassed is the tenant of a housing association or a local authority but the perpetrator may not be a tenant of the same landlord, or may be an owner occupier.

[26]This incident was powerfully reported in a BBC2 'Modern Times' documentary in April 1996, *Skin*.

Common misconceptions about racial harassment

Two of the most common misconceptions about harassment are that those experiencing harassment are not willing to report incidents to the police or give evidence
against the perpetrators. It is understandable that people
who are experiencing harassment may feel reluctant to
report cases to the police if they believe either that the
police will not turn up, or if they do, that they will not be
able or willing to do anything to stop it. In the worst case
scenario, the police may even arrest people seeking to
defend themselves or other members of their community.

For example, in October 1990 Mohammed Altaf was
acquitted of causing grievous bodily harm after defending his
sister from an armed white gang. No whites were charge.

In April 1992 armed white youths attacked a group of
Asians in Camden in London. The white group was later
outnumbered by Asians. Charges against members of the
white group were dropped. Three of the Asian youths
were tried and acquitted.

In fact, research indicates that many people experiencing harassment do in the first instance turn to the police.
In a survey conducted by Nottingham City Council 50 per
cent (66 of 133) of the cases had reported the harassment
to the police.[27] The work undertaken by the Community
Research Advisory Centre at the Polytechnic of North
London (now the University of North London) found
that all the victims of harassment had reported incidents

[27] Nottingham City Council (1992), *Racial harassment suffered by council tenants in the City of Nottingham.*

to the police.[28] The London Research Centre found in a report published in 1993 that one in ten ethnic minority households suffered racial attacks in and around the home. 51 per cent of these incidents had been reported to the police.[29]

People experiencing harassment may also fear that if they give evidence against perpetrators they will be targeted for further attack, not only by the original perpetrator, but by other people as well. This case study from Nottingham illustrates that possibility.

An elderly Pakistani couple, Mr and Mrs B, living in a house that they bought from the council under the right to buy scheme, suffered an extended, severe campaign of harassment which involved smashing all their windows, verbal abuse, damage to the car, racist graffiti, stones thrown at them and attempted arson. The main perpetrators were an 11-year-old boy and a 16-year-old girl.

The case was reported to the council at the beginning of June 1992. Following a swift, thorough investigation the council served notice two weeks later. When other local residents found out that court action was being considered, they too started being abusive towards Mr and Mrs B. The council approached various housing associations and asked them if they would consider purchasing Mr and Mrs B's property. A housing association duly bought the property and the couple moved to another area.

[28] Victim Support Racial Harassment Project.
[29] London Research Centre, *London Housing Survey 1992.*

The perpetrators' parents abandoned their property and presented themselves as homeless to another authority. The children were found sleeping in the back garden of their original home and were taken into care.[30]

Notwithstanding these extreme situations, this family was willing to give statements and appear in court. Research also supports the view that very many, though understandably not all, people who have been harassed were willing to give evidence. For example, the work done in Nottingham indicates that 51 per cent (68 of 133) were prepared to give evidence against perpetrators.

The way ahead

All of the incidents and cases above would have benefited from the involvement of a number of agencies — social landlords, the police, education authorities, social services, community groups etc. It is hard to imagine that the range of actions that need to be taken both to support the person being harassed and to ensure that the perpetrators desist can be achieved solely through the intervention of one agency.

In the light of this there has been much emphasis on the need for multi-agency working, which is discussed at greater length in chapter 2. Multi-agency working should ensure that all agencies have a much better picture of what is happening 'on the ground'. It should also give the

[30] Nottingham City Council 1992 *Racial harassment suffered by council tenants in the City of Nottingham.*

agencies involved a more effective coverage of changes in patterns of harassment that may develop over a period of time. Any patterns that do develop should inform not only action to be taken to resolve present problems, but also preventative action for the future, and the co-ordination of those actions at a neighbourhood or community level.

CHAPTER 2

THE MULTI-AGENCY APPROACH

Generally

Much of the research and good practice guidance on dealing with racial harassment since the first Home Affairs

Select Committee report has focused on the need for a multi-agency approach between the police, social landlords, social services, education authorities, community agencies etc. Whilst the argument for this approach in theory is irrefutable, in practice it has not always been so successful. However, the following is an example of successful multi-agency action.

Effective multi-agency action.[31]

A young Somali woman in South Glamorgan was seriously assaulted by a man and her house damaged during a neighbour dispute.

- The police quickly arrested the man.
- The local housing association was contacted and quickly effected repairs to the house.
- Social services was called in to support the victim and her family.
- The police explained the racial harassment aspect of the case to the Crown Prosecution Service.
- The Crown Prosecution Service added this to the evidence given in the prosecution of the man.

As a result the man received an 18-month prison sentence.[32]

[31] From *Racial Harassment in South Glamorgan*, the newsletter of South Glamorgan multi-agency forum on racial harassment.
[32] This leaflet was sent to the author. For other examples and references see *National Directory of Action Against Racial Harassment* (1996), Lemos & Crane.

The purpose of multi-agency working

The purpose of working with other agencies is to ensure that the authority and resources of a range of agencies are deployed in support of the person attacked, and in taking co-ordinated action against perpetrators. The 'hidden agenda' of multi-agency working can, cynically, be regarded as 'buck-passing', or shielding behind the inaction or incompetence of other organisations to defend an indifferent performance from the participant's own agency.

Many multi-agency groups are monitoring and review bodies. They thus tend to reflect only on what has happened. They do not intervene and take decisions about what needs to happen in individual cases. Nor do they plan and implement strategies for preventing harassment. They are not, in that sense, executive. There is, of course, a role for monitoring and review so long as it is focused towards improving future policy and practice in each and all of the participating agencies. Sometimes, however, discussion has been unfocused or defensive, and the deliberations of the multi-agency forum have either not been fed back into the participating agencies, or not implemented thereupon.

Another role for a multi-agency forum or group is deciding upon co-ordinated action to be taken in individual cases. This requires regular and frequent meetings of participants with the power both to take decisions and then to act upon them. The policy frameworks within which all the agencies work must 'fit together' – they should cross-refer, defining clear boundaries, not leaving gaps through which cases can fall. They should all be focused on the same outcome: identifying and acting in the best interest of person who has been attacked.

Local authorities cannot always convene the multi-agency forum, but a local authority's ability to weld together a coherent corporate approach is central to this process. Many of the authority's departments have a role to play. Without corporate direction it is easy for individual departments to establish their own policies and procedures which at best duplicate and at worst conflict with each other. Pooling information gathered by different departments may be particularly helpful in tracking down perpetrators.

The other well-defined role a multi-agency forum can play is to plan and execute a strategy for preventing racial harassment. It is this model that the Home Office has researched in North Plaistow and which is discussed in the next chapter (see page 49).[33]

Who should be involved in a multi-agency forum?

There are some obvious and key participants:

- the police
- the local authority, in particular as
  - social landlord
  - education authority

[33] Saulsbury W and Bowling B (1991), Home Office.

but also through its
- social services department
- legal department
- environmental health department
- other social landlords
- community advocates and agencies.

Other agencies that might be involved are:
- law centres
- local probation service.

The role of the police

Racial harassment is invariably and above all else a criminal matter. Many racially motivated incidents are either criminal damage or assaults. Because of their powers to investigate and recommend prosecution of criminal offences, the police are primarily concerned to deal with perpetrators. They can however make a substantial contribution to supporting those experiencing harassment.

The police need to demonstrate that they are sympathetic and believe both in what those experiencing racial harassment say and, more importantly, the racial motives behind the harassment. Police tardiness or failure to identify perpetrators and act against them will feed the black community's view that the police do not take the problem seriously and that it is therefore not worth reporting incidents. For example, the police and the Crown Prosecution Service were criticised by members of the black community after the death of Stephen Lawrence, an 18-year-old schoolboy at a bus stop, for not initiating a full-scale enquiry quickly enough and then not identifying enough evidence to prosecute the culprits.

Notwithstanding the above there is much that the police can do – and in some cases have done – more effectively to support those experiencing racial harassment. Specifically their actions need to:

- prevent harassment in the first place
- when it occurs, ensure it is reported to them
- take steps to improve the safety and sense of security of the person who has been attacked
- identify and initiate action against perpetrators of racial harassment.

Preventing harassment

Exhibition and display material used in the community can give positive messages both to people who may be the targets for racial attacks and to perpetrators about the police's willingness and ability to tackle this problem effectively. Crime prevention information can also be distributed. Where appropriate it can be translated into the main ethnic minority languages in the area.

Working with other agencies to increase reporting

The Metropolitan Police have recognised that lack of confidence in the police is sometimes a problem. Their guidance manual suggests:

'Where allegations of non-reporting are made, or where there are any real indications of lack of confidence in police or the reporting procedure, suitable voluntary organisations, statutory agencies and local authority departments (but not only those who are in all respects supportive of police) may be invited to become part of the reporting procedure.'[34]

South Yorkshire police comment that they have:

'close liaison with other organisations – e.g. the racial equality council for information about cultural aspects of individual cases and to enhance police officers' credibility with victims and overcome distrust of the police.'[35]

Supporting those experiencing harassment

Several police forces have introduced telephone helplines staffed by people who speak ethnic minority languages for people affected by racial violence. The resources for some of these helplines have come from commercial sponsorship. In South Wales police involvement in running the helplines is part of a multi-agency initiative.

In Bolton, Glasgow and elsewhere, the police are on standby to respond to calls coming through emergency telephone lines set up by the council housing departments for people being harassed. In Liverpool housing associations are planning to link their emergency alarms to police stations. Some police forces are taking the initiative – in Enfield, for example, police put in a joint bid with the

[34] Metropolitan Police (1990), *Working Together for Racial Harmony.*
[35] *National Directory of Action Against Racial Harassment* (1996), Lemos & Crane.

council social services department to extend the community alarm system.

The Metropolitan and South Yorkshire forces have bought into Language Line offering telephone interpreting in 140 languages. An incident can then be reported to the police via an interpreter. If a statement needs to be taken, arrangements can be made for an interpreter to be at the police station as soon as possible.

In Nottinghamshire, Divisional Community Affairs Sergeants visit people who have experienced racially motivated crime, to offer support and information, and to check the quality of the police response. There is a similar arrangement in South Yorkshire, while in Merseyside a 'victim liaison officer' is assigned to each serious case.

At the request of local authorities, there are numerous examples – from Croydon and Sandwell, to Kirklees and Newcastle – where police forces have increased patrolling and surveillance to protect individuals and targeted areas. In Rochdale, for people still feeling under threat of attack, this includes calling in to offer reassurance.[36]

Neighbourhood warning visits

In many areas an increase in the presence of the police or landlord's staff has led to a diminution in the number of attacks taking place. This raised profile gives a message of support to those who are experiencing harassment and to those who fear they might, as well as acting as a deterrent to potential perpetrators. It also gives a message to the wider

---

[36]Most of the examples come from the *National Directory of Action Against Racial Harassment* (1996), Lemos & Crane.

community about the determination of the authorities to clamp down on unacceptable and criminal behaviour.

Police action against perpetrators

There are a number of criminal legislative provisions under which the police can act against perpetrators who have been identified and about whom there is sufficient evidence. Housing managers do not need to know about them all in detail. It is nonetheless helpful to know the main ones. Assault and criminal damage are self-evident offences; it is also possible in some circumstances to prosecute for verbal abuse and threatening behaviour, both under the original Public Order Act 1986 and the more extensive provisions conferred by the Criminal Justice Act 1994. Incitement to racial hatred is an offence under the Race Relations Act 1976. This has been used to prosecute perpetrators of racial harassment who are motivated by far right political views.

As noted (page 28), people who are being attacked are more willing to involve the police and to give evidence than is commonly understood. This suggests that they are keen to see action taken – and that such action would make them feel safer and more protected.

Evidence

One of the most common reasons given by the police for not taking action is the difficulties of collecting adequate evidence to persuade the Crown Prosecution Service to pursue the case and to increase the likelihood of conviction in court.

It is important not to rely solely on the person who has

been harassed to provide the evidence. There may be known witnesses, or someone may be forthcoming if an appeal is made. Neighbours, residents' associations, neighbourhood watch, youth clubs and community organisations are all worth approaching. Estate based staff, especially caretakers, may have valuable information.

Surveillance operations are also possible, including the use of audio tape, photography, video and closed circuit TV. Volunteers sometimes stay overnight at the homes of people under persistent attack, while private investigators and professional witnesses have, in extreme cases, been used to stake out homes which are regularly targeted.[37]

There is, nonetheless, an inevitable need for the person who has been attacked to be able to provide evidence in some cases.

Specialist officers and teams

Many forces contain specialist officers or teams. Generally specialist staff have more information, understanding and sympathy in cases of racial harassment. Housing managers would do well to ensure that they know whether there are any specialist staff in their area, who they are, how they can be contacted and what is in their remit. It is obviously best if they have that information before an attack occurs, not after.

---

[37] Examples of all these methods of collecting evidence can be found in the *National Directory of Action Against Racial Harassment* (1996), Lemos & Crane.

The role of the local authority

As strategic planner

Within most local authorities the Chief Executive's department has a central planning role. It is ideally placed to ensure that all relevant departments develop policies and procedures on racial harassment and that these fit into an overall corporate strategy. In this way, policies are consistent across departments and all relevant information is accessible and exchangeable. With a clear corporate strategy, the authority is then well placed to work with other organisations in a multi-agency approach. In practice this is unlikely to be achieved without a clear commitment from elected members.

As social landlord and housing authority

The authority's role as a social landlord is covered in *Eliminating Racial Harassment – a guide to housing policies and procedures*. Through its housing advice role, an authority may also be called on to support those living in privately rented housing, and even owner occupiers.

Housing departments are thus often at the forefront of a local authority's work in supporting those experiencing harassment, with much thought being put into their working practice. Often, however, the very intensity of this work means there is less consideration given to inter-department liaison, and to corporate strategy.

As education authority

The perpetrators of many incidents of racial harassment

are young people who are still at school, and harassment which may be occurring in the home also often takes place in the school or the playground, as well as on the street. In the school setting it is far more likely that perpetrators can be identified.

However, there is a risk that the policies for dealing with this may not harmonise with those of social landlords. To take an extreme example: a school may exclude temporarily a pupil who persistently bullies or harasses black or ethnic minority pupils. Without getting the pupil's family to co-operate in the sanctions used, there is a risk that the young perpetrator might attack people in their home or on the street if he or she is at liberty with nothing to occupy him or her. Whilst the school's problem may have been temporarily solved or averted, the problem of harassment has merely been moved, not ended.

County schools are now locally managed, so the governors of each school are responsible for drawing up the policy on racial harassment. However, there is still a crucial role for each local education authority in ensuring that this happens. Each authority should:

- distribute a draft policy to every governing body
- monitor schools to see that a policy is being adopted
- ask for all incidents to be reported to the authority centrally, so that incidents in school can be related to activity outside, and to any multi-agency initiative
- provide training in policy adoption
- offer advisers who will go out and discuss the issue in schools.

There are several key elements to any policy guidelines:

- There should be a whole school approach in drawing them up – involving governors, teachers, support staff, parents and the children themselves
- Prevention should be prioritised. Many schools build this into their curriculum development with specific projects and such things as poster and poetry competitions
- Strategies for supporting students being harassed and for taking action against perpetrators need to be linked into the school's behaviour, anti-bullying and equal opportunities policies. Such policies should always clearly establish which adult a student can rely on for pastoral care, and what sanctions are to be brought to bear if the policy is ignored.

Some schools are now pioneering training for students in anti-bullying strategies. This makes clear that they have a responsibility to act where they see others being bullied or harassed, and gives them techniques for offering confidential peer group support and counselling for children subjected to bullying.

The playground is often where harassment occurs. Schools should fully value their playground supervisory staff and train them properly. At South Camden Community School in London all supervisors are ex-students with youth training qualifications. This has proved extremely effective in getting early warning of potential conflict.

As law enforcer

Local authority legal departments have been much criticised for their caution and their unwillingness to take action against perpetrators. In September 1990 *Legal Action* published the results of a survey by Lee Bridges and Duncan Forbes which looked into the way local authority legal departments were handling racial harassment cases. This highlighted common problems:

1. Housing departments present cases far too late, when they have gone stale, and with inadequate statements.
2. Housing staff were unaware of what legal remedies were available.
3. Procedures linking the legal department into the housing department's work were lacking. Often it was unclear who was responsible for progressing which elements of a case to court. Who was responsible for collecting witness statements? Were they trained to do it?
4. There was little prioritisation of the work within legal departments with lawyers sometimes deciding to take no action even where this conflicted with policy decisions made by councillors.

It would therefore be to everyone's benefit if legal departments could be involved at an early stage, advising on the handling of cases, as well as ensuring the right evidence is collected in a way that is acceptable to a court. The *Legal Action* survey mentioned above contains a detailed Code of Guidance on this.[38]

As provider of social services
Social services departments sometimes support people

---

[38]Legal Action Group (1990) *Making the Law Work Against Racial Harassment.*

who have been harassed and are in distress. They have responsibility under the Children Act to ensure the well-being of children affected by the harassment.

Social services may be involved with perpetrators in a counselling role. They may also need to exercise Children Act responsibilities here. The Act may, for example, have an impact on the handling of possession proceedings against families with children. Again early involvement is beneficial.

In some cases, families responsible for harassment may already be known to social services. In discussing what action to take, particularly against young offenders, this history may be of value. Although, in general, social services has a duty not to divulge information, there may be circumstances in which this is appropriate.

As enforcer of environmental health standards

Environmental health departments can also assist in, for example, controlling harassment caused by noise or rubbish dumping. They have to take care that they do not unwittingly collude in harassment. There have been cases of perpetrators maliciously complaining to environmental health departments about people they are harassing. The Commission for Racial Equality has recently published a guide on these issues.[39]

The role of other social landlords

Housing associations' policies and procedures for dealing with cases differ little from those of local authorities.

---

[39] *Environmental Health and Racial Equality* (1995), Commission for Racial Equality.

Associations are mainly concerned about harassment directed at their own tenants. Many housing associations do not have their stock concentrated on large estates so tenants being harassed may be isolated and perpetrators frequently have no connection with the association. To expand the range of support for those being harassed, and to widen the options for dealing with perpetrators, involvement with a multi-agency group is of great benefit.

The role of community agencies

People experiencing harassment often turn to community agencies when they have become tired and frustrated by what they perceive to be the supine inactivity of authorities such as landlords and police. Whilst community agencies have certainly been effective in increasing the number of cases that are reported, and have in some instances mobilised effective community and collective responses, they do not have the power to act against perpetrators in a way that will make them desist from further harassment. For this, they need to co-operate with the authorities.

Multi-agency forums easily become places where active community agencies with limited power are voluble in their denunciations of inaction on the authorities' part. This may be cathartic, and in the short run exert necessary pressure. In the long run, however, co-operation not confrontation is needed.[40]

---

[40] Many examples of effective responses from community agencies, including SARI in Bristol and Newham Monitoring Project, are given in the *National Directory of Action Against Racial Harassment* (1996), Lemos & Crane.

The role of other agencies

Law centres often advise or act for people who have been attacked and who have failed to get adequate action from the police or the landlord. They may also assist people who have been attacked in taking action themselves. Some law centres have extended their brief to preventative work.

Probation services may be involved with perpetrators if they are on probation for a previous offence, related or otherwise. They have a counselling role – ideally to intervene positively with perpetrators – as well as the legal duty to take action if the probation order is breached. If the probation order prohibits approaching a particular family or property, or prohibits harassment, housing managers need to work closely with the probation officer to ensure that possible breaches are reported and acted upon.

CHAPTER 3

MULTI-AGENCY WORKING IN PRACTICE: A CASE STUDY

The North Plaistow Racial Harassment
Project / *Problem description / Devising an
action plan / Implementation and evaluation:
successes and failures* / Recommendations for
future multi-agency efforts

The North Plaistow Racial Harassment Project

Multi-agency working is not easy. The North Plaistow
Racial Harassment Project is a good example of the problems that are likely to be encountered and provides useful
lessons for future work.[41] The Home Office initiated the
project in 1987, as one response to the 1986 Home Affairs
Select Committee report. Its progress was carefully moni-
tored by Home Office researchers.

North Plaistow is in the east London Borough of

---

[41]The project has been fully written up by Saulsbury W and Bowling B, and their
findings published by the Home Office.

Newham. Although Newham is an Outer London borough, its social, economic and environmental conditions display many inner city characteristics. In terms of housing and unemployment the borough contains some of the most deprived areas in the country.

A significant proportion of the population of North Plaistow (well over the 20 per cent average in the 1991 census for Greater London) is black or from an ethnic minority, including large Asian and African Caribbean populations. About half of the residents rent from the council. There are many tower blocks in the area. In its submission to the Department of the Environment, the local authority said estates like Brooks Road were characterised by 'crime, fear of crime, vandalism, racial harassment, squatting, noisy parties, rent arrears and the alienation of the tenants from their environment'.

The narrow, eastern end of the project area is within one of the centres of Newham's several Asian communities. It is comprised mainly of owner-occupied terraced houses. Some are privately rented.

The North Plaistow project brought together in 1987 the Metropolitan Police, the London Borough of Newham, Newham Council for Racial Equality, Victim Support Newham and the Home Office. The project's aims were to:

• monitor recent racial harassment and attacks
• assist victims
• identify and take action against perpetrators
• tackle under-reporting of incidents by more efficient use of existing resources

- develop more effective co-operation between the agencies involved.

The project had three stages: problem description; devising an action plan; and implementation and evaluation.

Problem description

A high proportion of those interviewed in the research on the effectiveness of the multi-agency approach considered racial harassment to be one of the area's problems:

Percentage of North Plaistow's population who thought racial harassment was either a 'big' or a 'bit of a' problem

	Women	Men
Asian	51	50
African & Afro-Caribbean	38	29
White	16	26

In terms of the types of attacks that were taking place, many of the patterns already discussed emerged in this research. Significantly, 95 per cent of the people attacked were generally dissatisfied with the authorities' response.

Devising an action plan

Having defined the problems an action plan covering the following areas was devised:

A. Prevention of incidents

This included addressing the underlying causes by cleaning up the area, co-ordinating the maintenance of an improved environment and crime prevention through initiatives such as area lighting. Targeted police patrols were recommended as a way of discouraging incidents.

B. Reducing fear of victimisation

This covered some of the initiatives already discussed as well as police outreach programmes to community groups.

C. Encouraging reporting of incidents

Apart from the police outreach programme, there was also a schools student poster campaign recommended, as well as newspaper publicity, and a local meeting on the action plan. There was also action to make reporting easier through a pilot scheme carried out in schools.

D. Assisting victims

This area of the plan was divided between immediate support, follow-up and long-term support networks. Immediate support should come from the first police officer at the incident, with a follow-up visit from the home beat officer. There should also be a swift response from housing officers. A co-ordinated information package was also going to be produced.

The police and the housing department were to make referrals to the local victim support scheme for follow-up support. In the long term there should be a network of volunteer supporters organised by the housing department and the local victim support scheme.

E. Identifying perpetrators

The project wanted to improve the chances of identifying perpetrators both at the time of the incident and through follow-up investigation. For immediate identification, the first police officer to attend should make a fuller investigation and the housing staff should also encourage people who had been attacked to identify perpetrators.

CID could be involved in identifying perpetrators through follow-up investigation, while housing staff could canvas for witnesses.

F. Action against perpetrators

A greater emphasis would be placed on deterrence through issuing warnings and, where appropriate, counselling. Schools would need to adopt good practice guidelines for counselling perpetrators while the housing department would have to improve its monitoring of incidents and its responsiveness.

G. Improving inter-agency co-operation

Enhanced channels of communication and better co-ordination of support for victims were needed. Channels of communication would improve through regular informal meetings between the police and the housing department. The co-ordination of support for victims could come through some of the initiatives already mentioned, for example the volunteer support network, the referrals to victim support and the co-ordinated information package.

H. Improving single agency response

Improved training for both housing and police officers was needed. This could also be addressed through police assessment of victim satisfaction, the housing department racial incident panel decision-making and the schools anti-racist committee.

Implementation and evaluation: successes and failures

The North Plaistow multi-agency group's experience would undoubtedly be encountered in other areas. Fast upon a sense of relief that something was at last being done about a long-standing problem came the raising of expectations, ultimately to unachievable levels. That was the first limitation on the project. It resulted in an attempt to tackle all aspects of the problem at once.

Another limitation was that the group's members did not have the authority to make an impact. The Crown Prosecution Service was, for example, unwilling to participate. Uncertainty about the availability of resources was also a crucial limiting factor. These problems and others could be said to be outside the remit of the participants in the multi-agency group.

But some of the limiting factors were within their control. For example, the extensive information gathering exercise about the problem's spread, nature and location was not then used to target the police outreach programme to community groups. Given the findings, this could usefully have been targeted at Asian women's groups.

The group also avoided initiatives which they believed to be difficult to organise or to have untenable resource implications, with the result that some initiatives, for example on preventing attacks, were limited to the fairly obvious – targeted police patrols, improved street lighting and an area clean-up. There was no discussion of a more positive intervention with perpetrators, which might have been achieved through the probation service, the youth service or leisure services.

The researchers identified another limitation:

> '. . . there was a lack of concerted engagement displayed in the working group's deliberations about considering, recommending or shepherding clear changes to established procedures. It appeared that "middle of the road" initiatives were put forward because they did not risk seriously upsetting the status quo between involved agencies or between different parts of a particular agency.'

This detailed research provides lessons for all forms of multi-agency working, as these limitations are frequently encountered.

Recommendations for future multi-agency efforts

The Home Office researchers recommended improvements to the effectiveness of multi-agency working. Included were proposals to:

- clearly identify the benefits of multi-agency working for all parties involved

- set clear goals, an operational plan and an achievable schedule
- recognise that there will be a need for substantive work by some if not all the agencies involved in the project; this has resource and workload implications with the possible need for full- or part-time secondment
- recognise that the multi-agency project will need to be financially supported
- set up clear arrangements for reporting back to participating agencies
- have an independent chair
- identify a clear role for the steering group, as distinct from the role of each participating agency
- use task or working groups to initiate and complete particular pieces of work, which the steering group can monitor
- recognise that the project is likely to result in the participating organisations needing to review their own internal policies, procedures and practices
- set up clear monitoring arrangements.

PART II

PRACTICE

CHAPTER 4

EXPECTATIONS OF PEOPLE EXPERIENCING HARASSMENT

People who experience racial harassment clearly feel that not enough is being done (as shown in the research that has been carried out in Nottingham, Birmingham and North Plaistow – see chapters 1-3). So landlords, the police and education authorities are therefore advised to make a clear statement, an undertaking of what tenants have a right to expect should they be targets for racial attacks. This should be seen in the wider context of service providers stating explicitly the standards that their customers and service users can expect and the redress available when these standards are not met. This is the principle of the Citizens' Charter to which many local authorities and police forces have subscribed.

Below is a list of minimum expectations. If incorporated into policy by social landlords, the police and education authorities this could form the basis of an agreement which should both raise standards of service and boost the low levels of tenant confidence. This, in turn, would make it more likely that attacks are perhaps prevented, certainly reported earlier, and possibly dealt with more effectively.

Expectations of people experiencing racial harassment
Tenants will expect the landlord and other agencies:

- To take the problem seriously.
- To listen to and believe not only what has happened to them, but also why.
- To provide a trained independent interpreter if English is not their first language, and not to expect the tenants themselves to provide their own interpreter or to use relatives or children.
- To welcome tenants' advocates.
- To respect confidentiality and anonymity both within the agency or authority, and in discussion with perpetrators, other tenants and other organisations.
- To acknowledge and validate tenants' feelings and fears, and not to minimise or ignore them.
- To repair damage caused by harassment in the shortest possible time – 24 hours for emergencies.
- To have the home secured at the landlord's expense.
- To improve home security if necessary.
- To act on incidents reported to the police.
- To offer the same level of help even where tenants do not feel it is safe to report incidents to the police.
- To take action as landlord to stop perpetrators whenever the perpetrator is a tenant of the same landlord.
- To take action against perpetrators even if they are not tenants of the same landlord.
- To support tenants wanting to stay in their own home.

- To rehouse a tenant as soon as possible, either temporarily or permanently, if that tenant feels the harassment is intolerable.
- To offer a new home to a tenant who is forced to move which is neither smaller, nor in a less suitable area, nor with fewer facilities than the one they are leaving.
- To bear the costs of the move which the tenant did not initially want to make. Costs should be borne by the landlord, or sought from the perpetrator.
- To give a tenant the right to move back home once the threat of harassment is over, if they were moved out temporarily.
- To work together co-operatively with other agencies in the best interest of the tenant as the tenant defines it.
- To keep the tenant informed.
- To take no action without the tenant's consent.
- To take action against the perpetrator to stop the harassment, whether or not the tenant is willing to give evidence in court.
- To ensure the safety and security of the school and the playground.
- To take effective action to stop bullying and harassment between pupils in the school, in the playground or on the way to and from school.

CHAPTER 5

ENSURING RACIAL ATTACKS ARE REPORTED

Publicising policies for dealing with racial harassment / Tenants' associations / Community development work / The role of other tenants / *Newsletters and meetings / Other tenants as witnesses /* Advocates / Advising tenants of steps they should take when encountering racial harassment / Signing up procedures / Involvement of non-housing management staff / The role of specialist staff

Most racial attacks are not reported; possible reasons for this are examined in Part I. So organisations that are serious about taking action against racial harassment, and supporting those experiencing it, need to ensure that they take all available steps to encourage reporting.

This chapter makes some suggestions about how to increase the level of reporting. The remainder of the book is concerned with ways of giving effective support to those under attack. The two are related. If authorities are consistently effective in giving support to those being harassed, this is quickly recognised through informal networks, and it encourages others who are suffering the same experiences to report what is happening.

Publicising policies for dealing with racial harassment

Leaflets, posters, videos and cassette recordings have all been used by organisations to publicise their policies to those who may potentially experience racial harassment. They should cover what to do if people are attacked, who they can report it to, and from whom they may get support. This has not just been the role of landlords, schools or the police. Community organisations and victim support schemes have played a major role.

These publicity campaigns are important initiatives:

- They give a specific message to people who fear harassment that they can do something about it should they experience it.
- They give a wider message to the community that the agency – either the landlord or another organisation – takes the problem seriously. This should be a deterrent to putative perpetrators.
- They should be a reminder to perpetrators' friends and acquaintances of the effects of racial harassment and the need for them to report any incidents they know of.
- They convey to perpetrators that they would be well

advised in this particular area not to carry out racial attacks. Should they do so they are likely to face serious consequences, as a result of action either by the landlord or by the police.

A case in 1994 in the East End of London was brought by the police against one of a group of white youths who had attacked an Asian youth, using his head as a football. Identification of one of the culprits was as a result of a white girl with whom he had been out once or twice, and to whom he boasted about the attack, going to the police. This kind of action, where members of the community assist in identifying and isolating perpetrators, is a most welcome recent development in the fight against racial attacks and harassment.

The consequences of this girl's courageous actions, for which she won an award, were in some ways unfortunate. She was ostracised at school and even abused for her 'betrayal'. In the end, she found herself having to make new friends and a life outside the area. This conspiracy of prejudice and silence amongst those who may not themselves commit racial attacks but who shield and excuse those who do, is the nourishment on which the problem feeds and is sustained. It can be seen by perpetrators as pleasurable acts of violence and aggression, for which there are no retributive consequences, at least so far as they are concerned.[42]

---

[42] This young woman's experiences were graphically recounted in the BBC2 Cutting Edge documentary *Skin* in April 1996.

Tenants associations

The Government, local authorities and housing associations are keen to encourage the participation of tenants in the management of their own housing. One form of involvement is through the formation of tenants associations. Landlords need to ensure that when tenants associations are formed they are genuinely representative of all the communities living on an estate or in a neighbourhood. If vulnerable or excluded groups are not represented then such associations are unlikely to be an effective forum for the sharing of information about attacks and harassment; neither are they likely to be sources of support for those who are experiencing harassment.

Traditionally the places the tenants associations have met and the ways in which they have conducted their business have been either intimidating or off-putting to tenants of ethnic minority groups, as well as to women and people with disabilities. It is not only having a representative membership that is important, it is also the group's attitudes and behaviour that should be inclusive.

Much concern has been expressed that tenants associations are themselves the source of aid, succour and support to the perpetrators of harassment. A BBC documentary[43] charted the involvement of a tenants association and the activities in a tenants' hall on an estate in Hounslow in the racial harassment of a local Asian shopkeeper and his family. In that instance many of the youths who used the

---

[43] *Intolerance*, BBC.

facilities, particularly the youth group, had their mis-
demeanours ignored by the people who ran the association.
Perhaps even worse, the leaders of the group, though not
themselves perpetrators of racial harassment, often sought
to give explanations or justifications for physical attacks on
people and property. The tenants association members
were both passively and actively colluding in the attacks
and harassment.

An effective strategy for ensuring that cases of racial
harassment are reported and that where possible racial harassment is prevented will ensure that tenants associations
are genuinely representative. Tenants associations can then:

- adopt anti-racist and anti-harassment positions as a way
  of showing support for people experiencing racial
  harassment
- help provide the practical support of neighbours and the
  local community – especially important as many incidents of harassment occur outside
- build the confidence of potential witnesses, who may
  themselves have experienced other forms of nuisance
  from perpetrators
- change the climate of opinion on an estate, making it
  feel a safer place to live and making perpetrators feel
  like the criminals they are.

A film forming part of the 'Mosaic' series,[44] gives an
example of a tenants association in Coventry, made up of
tenants from different racial groups who began to work

[44] *Living in Fear*, BBC.

together effectively to combat racial harassment. But the strategy was successful only once the worst perpetrators had been removed from the estate and that racially divisive influence had gone.[45]

Community development work

Community development can help prevent racial harassment and support those experiencing it. This links in with the issues surrounding work with tenants associations and tenants' participation. Community development work can:

- ensure that everybody who lives in a particular community is aware of potential problems experienced by its vulnerable members
- establish local structures and organisations and support systems such as voluntary help lines and witness support schemes to ensure that people experiencing harassment get some support
- provide help in identifying perpetrators of racial harassment so that action can be taken against them
- identify potential advocates for people experiencing racial harassment
- ensure that black and white tenants work together, so that those who have been racially attacked, or fear that they might be, do not regard all the white people in an area or on an estate as potential attackers, thus magnifying their fears.

[45] The role of tenants associations in combating racial harassment is discussed in more detail in *Eliminating Racial Harassment: a guide to policies and procedures* (1994), Lemos & Crane.

The role of other tenants

Landlords and other authorities need to make it clear to all their tenants, not just those who might be the targets for racial attacks, or the perpetrators, what their policy is on racial harassment. Tenants who are not themselves involved can play an active role in reporting incidents, providing support, and isolating and discouraging perpetrators.

Newsletters and meetings

Tenants' newsletters and tenants' meetings or forums are all good ways to do this. The key messages that housing managers will want to convey are:

- the landlord takes the problem seriously
- the landlord will do everything possible to support those experiencing harassment
- tenants should report incidents when they encounter them, even if they are not the person who has been attacked or harassed
- where perpetrators are identified and evidence has been gathered, action will be taken against them.

Newsletters are also a good place to publicise cases that have been dealt with effectively, and also more generally to include positive images and messages about the fact that the estate or area is multi-racial, and that the landlord welcomes that.

Other tenants as witnesses

Some possession cases have failed in the courts as being

not proved. The point has been made several times: good evidence is needed if action is to be successful. Apart from the person who has been attacked, and anyone who witnessed the incident by chance, there is also a role for other tenants, alongside the police and security services if they exist, to keep a more systematic eye out for harassment or other forms of nuisance, take a proper record, and report it as quickly as possible.

Advocates

The role of advocates is described fully in chapter 8. Research in Birmingham[46] suggests that for someone experiencing harassment, an advocate increases the likelihood of a satisfactory outcome. The involvement of advocates through the Newham Monitoring Project and the Southall Monitoring Project (both in London) and SARI in Bristol[47] has also led to a much higher incidence of reporting of harassment in their local areas, compared with surrounding areas where it is likely that the problem is just as bad if not worse.

[46] *The support needs of tenants suffering racial harassment – findings and recommendations of a research survey*, Birmingham City Council Housing Department (1993).
[47] See the *National Directory of Actions Against Racial Harassment* (1996), Lemos & Crane for more details of these examples.

Advising tenants of the steps they should take in the event of encountering racial harassment

Too often people who have experienced racial harassment have not known that any support is on offer at all, whether from their landlord, the police or from local community organisations. As a response to this many police forces have produced information for tenants encouraging them to report racial attacks. Local authorities too have provided written information. Other initiatives that have been taken are telephone helplines where people can find out what they should do if they are attacked and specialist support staff who are estate-based and therefore can act as a source of information.

Signing up procedures

If preventing racial harassment is to be regarded as a core activity of a social housing management service it is important that those people who are primarily responsible for the service, i.e. the housing managers themselves, take an active role in ensuring that those who might experience racial harassment know what they should do if there are any problems. The most appropriate time to do this is when they sign the tenancy agreement.

At the signing up session housing managers will want to ensure that new tenants know of their rights and duties under the tenancy agreement, and fully understand the landlord's role. Alongside the more obvious messages about rent payments and arrears and arrangements for reporting repairs, housing managers would also do well to draw the new tenants' attention to a clause in the tenancy agreement which states that by harassing their neighbours they may lose their home, and if they are attacked they can depend on the landlord's support when they report the incident.

Involvement of non-housing management staff

Many incidents of racial harassment come to light not as a result of a report of a racial incident, but as a result of either a transfer request to the landlord or a request for repairs to be done. It is therefore important that the staff who deal with these other matters are aware of the possibilities of racial harassment lurking behind the presenting issue.

Training clearly has a role to play here. It should be provided for all staff in recognising harassment, knowing the organisation's policy on harassment, and knowing what their role is in reporting incidents of harassment – what they should say to the tenants, to whom they should report incidents, and in what format. If the organisation has a form they will obviously need to know about it – where to find it, how to fill it in and to whom it should be sent.[48]

[48]Training on dealing with racial harassment is discussed fully in *Eliminating Racial Harassment: a guide to policies and procedures*, Lemos G (1994), Lemos & Crane.

The role of specialist staff

In chapter 8 various initiatives for employing specialist staff are discussed. Inevitably, much of the work of specialist staff focuses on casework after attacks or incidents of racial harassment have been reported – either in supporting those who have experienced the attack or in taking action against perpetrators.

There is also a useful role for specialist staff in ensuring that incidents are reported. This links to community development work. Visiting local people and community groups, both black and white, explaining the nature of the problem, the authority's policy and their role as specialist staff gives a message of support to those who might be experiencing the attacks, or might potentially experience them, and a message of deterrence to perpetrators. It also give a message to other tenants to encourage them to support those experiencing harassment, to report incidents that they witness and to act as witnesses in the event of a case against a perpetrator being taken.

Many successful actions against perpetrators of racial harassment have involved witnesses who have not themselves been the targets of racial attacks. They have either given evidence of what they have witnessed, or confirmed that the perpetrators have also caused a nuisance to them.[49]

---

[49]This was a feature of the very first successful prosecution widely reported – the McDonalds in Newham. There are other examples in *Racial Attacks and Harassment: the response of social landlords*, (1996) London Research Centre for the DoE, HMSO.

CHAPTER 6

INTERVIEWING SKILLS

Empowerment / Empathy / Risks of bad
interviews / *Sympathetic over-identification /
Confrontational questioning* / The best interests
of the person who has been attacked / Power
in the interview / Techniques / *Listening /
Active silence / Pace of the interview / Verbal
and non-verbal messages / Seeking advice
on body language / Questioning /
Summarising and reflecting* / Use of
interpreters / Note-taking

It is now widely accepted that the manner in which representatives of authority, such as the police, conduct
interviews has a critical impact on the support that the
person who has been attacked feels they are receiving,
their ability to make decisions for themselves about what
is in their best interest, and ultimately whether they will
co-operate in any action the authority might take, such
as criminal prosecution or possession proceedings.

Social workers handling cases of abuse or violence have
long been aware of the danger of a poorly conducted interview leaving the person who has been attacked feeling

worse than before the 'helper' arrived. The police have also changed the way they investigate rape and domestic violence. For example, interviews and investigations are now more often conducted by women police officers, and the interviewing techniques are more gentle and supportive. The lessons learnt in these instances are no less applicable in dealing with cases of racial harassment.

This chapter outlines the key skills that interviewers need to conduct effective interviews. These skills are equally applicable to social workers, police officers, housing managers and teachers.

Empowerment

The victim-centred approach has been a feature of many policies and procedures for dealing with harassment. This has reduced the number of occasions when people who have been attacked are disbelieved, or have their motives questioned. Yet it does not always lead to a more positive approach being taken to supporting them.

Empowerment is perhaps an over-used and clichéd word. It may also, at first glance, be difficult to see its relevance to someone who has been harassed or attacked. In fact, empowerment is most important in situations where someone is feeling powerless and overcome by events that they cannot predict or control.

It is not suggested here that people who have been attacked should take revenge, or take the law into their own hands; neither should they be left to deal with the situation on their own. However, people who have been harassed *can* be empowered through:

- ensuring that they define what is in their best interest
- knowing of all the available options
- making informed choices
- controlling what is done both by themselves and others on their behalf.

The alternative is that the approach of those charged with helping, such as the landlord, the police or the education authorities, will not help. It may in fact make the situation worse, because they are insensitive, indifferent, heavy-handed or because their conduct of investigations comes to form part of the attack on the person being harassed.

Empathy

The interviewer should first and foremost be supportive to the person who has been attacked, but should also remain objective and clear-sighted throughout the interview. In order to do this they need to ensure that they seek to see the incidents through the eyes and in the way of the person who has experienced the harassment. The question the interviewer needs to ask themselves is not 'How would I feel if this was happening to me?', but 'How would I feel if I was this person and this was happening to me?'.

It is obviously not possible to see the world through someone else's eyes, but there is usually some indication from an interviewer's own experience that can provide some insight into how the other person might be feeling. The experience of discrimination, harassment or attacks happens to all kinds of people, not just on the grounds of race. Interviewers therefore should be aware of their own experience of harassment as a source of insight. It is unwise, however, to assume that their own experience is the same or sufficiently similar and simply to use that as a transferable template of what the person who has been attacked feels or needs.

Risks of bad interviews

Sympathetic over-identification
Sympathetic over-identification may lead to outcomes which the person being harassed did not want: such outcomes do not help because they are not being controlled by the supposed beneficiary.

Don't say	'I know how you feel as a black woman myself'
	'I know just what it's like to be harassed'
Do say	'How have these incidents affected you?'

This ability to show empathy is essential to a successful outcome of the interview. Unwelcome outcomes of badly conducted interviews (which lack a sense of empathy) are that the person harassed feels they are not being listened to, or they are not getting a full chance to explain themself, or not getting offered any practical support.

In over-identifying with the person attacked perhaps as a result of their own previous experience, the interviewer is in danger of considering not how they would feel if they were the person under attack, but how they would feel if it had happened to them. They would be experiencing vicarious responses to the incident, feeling conflicts of fear, guilt, anger and powerlessness.

If the interviewer is white, and of the same racial group as the perpetrator, they may feel guilt or some responsibility for the actions of a member of their group. A black interviewer may, on the other hand, be filled with a sense of outrage and anger at what has happened to someone like them. Both responses are understandable, and possibly not easy to avoid, but should nonetheless be contained so that they do not affect the interview's conduct or outcome.

In both scenarios, the result is the same.

Don't say	'Something like that has happened to me. I felt terrible. That's made me more determined to sort these people out.'
	'This kind of behaviour really makes me angry. I'll do everything possible to look after you.'
	'I'll make sure they don't do it again.'
Do say	'I know when things like this happen it can be really upsetting, so we are here to do what we can to support you.'

Do say	'My job is to make sure that you're fully in the picture about what can be done, so that you can decide what happens next.'
	'We won't go ahead with anything unless you agree with it.'
	'I'll make sure you know exactly what's happening. I will come around in a week's time to tell you how I've got on.'
Don't say	'Do you want me to do anything else?'
	'Is there anything else that I can help you to do?'
Do say	'If you need to know anything else, or there is anything more you think we should be doing, here's where to contact me.'

The danger here is that the interviewer might adopt the following mind-set: because such a terrible thing has happened, there is nothing that the person who has been attacked can do for themselves. They become more victim-like in the interviewer's mind, and indeed in their own mind. The incident itself would have brought up feelings of guilt, anger and powerlessness. The interview may inadvertently reinforce these feelings.

An overly-sympathetic approach means that the person being interviewed feels taken over and that there is nothing that they can do to help themself, and so they must leave everything to the interviewer as a representative of power and authority. Apart from the inappropriate feelings of powerlessness, this may also raise unrealistic expectations in the mind of the person harassed about what practically can be done.

Confrontational questioning

Where the person being interviewed feels their word is doubted they will feel that they, and not the perpetrator, are having to defend themself, or prove that the incident took place at all. They may even feel that they have to prove that the attack happened in the way that they say it did, for the motives they ascribe, or had the effect on them or their family that they say it had.

Don't say	'Are you sure it wasn't just kids messing about?'
	'These kinds of things happen to all sorts of people around here – black and white.'
	'Are you sure your kids weren't involved as well?'
Do say	'This sort of thing can be very frightening. How did you feel?'
	'Has it affected your family in any other ways?'

If the person who has been attacked has given no indication of what they think the motive for the attack might be:

Do say	'Do you think you were being specifically targeted for any reason?'

Inappropriately conducted interviews can be part of the problem of harassment, not the solution. If questioning by the interviewer is too direct, harsh or confrontational, the person being interviewed will feel that the attack is coming jointly from the perpetrator *and* the interviewer.

The best interests of the person who has been attacked

The experience of racial harassment can be traumatic and may leave the person who has been attacked feeling panicky and anxious that something should be done, or that they themself should do something. Research by Birmingham City Council Housing Department confirms that people being racially harassed either feel aggressive and angry or powerless and frightened, or their feelings fluctuate between these poles.

These feelings have in many cases manifested themselves as requests for a transfer to another property. Taken at face value, this may be thought to be a considered expression of the tenant's conclusion about where their best interests lie.

In fact, they may wish to stay in their existing home so long as the unacceptable behaviour is stopped. They may also not, once they have considered the matter further, continue to believe that moving is what is best for them. Moving might involve children changing schools; social, religious and community networks being severed; additional expense and an unacceptably high level of stress. The interviewer has to establish what the tenant really feels, and what they feel would be in their best interest, having considered all the available options.

This should always be the interviewer's primary concern. The tenant's best interest should be as they define it themself, once they have been given all the relevant information, not as defined by the interviewer, another agency, a relative or any other party.

Whilst this principle is easy to enunciate, it is considerably harder to enact. The person may not know what is in their best interest. They may be looking for guidance. They may quite legitimately be influenced by others that they trust or by those that they perceive as having their best interests at heart, but who are far from objective. In some circumstances this may apply to relatives.

All these factors make it difficult for the housing manager to ensure that what the tenant is expressing as being what they want, is in fact a decision that has been reached after consideration of all the available options, and is not likely to change on further reflection.

The interviewer should ensure that the person experiencing harassment:

- feels supported
- has considered all the available options
- has decided what is in their best interest.

As interviewer, they need to be sure they:

- have clearly heard and understood what happened and why
- know how the person attacked feels
- are clear about what that person wants to happen as a result.

Power in the interview

Interviewers should be continually conscious of the power inequality between themselves and the person being interviewed. This inequality is born of several factors. First the interviewer is the landlord's representative and is vested with the power of the landlord. Secondly, the person has been attacked and is likely to feel an increased sense of vulnerability and powerlessness. Lastly responsibility for the conduct of the interview is vested with the interviewer. All of the interviewer's behaviour and questioning should be conducted with a mind to acknowledge and minimise these inequalities.

It is obviously not appropriate constantly to remind the person harassed of their powerlessness or inequality. But the interviewer can, through their listening skills and willingness to assist and support, through their approach to the questioning, the interview's structure and the clarity of their ground rules, implicitly acknowledge and respond to the needs of the person harassed, and thereby reduce the inequality.

Don't say	'There isn't much you can do here, is there?'
	'Leave it to us. We'll sort it out.'
	'I've got some questions you need to answer before I can do anything.'
Do say	'We will do what we can to help once we have discussed what you feel is best.'

Techniques

Listening

To say interviewers should listen to what is being said to them is a banal statement of the obvious. To do this effectively the interviewer needs not only to hear the words that the person being interviewed uses, but clearly to understand the messages they wish to convey. This will require them to listen carefully, give clear signals, both verbally and non-verbally, that they have heard what is being said, ask open questions in a structured way, follow up those questions in a way that is both supportive and probing, and clearly reflect back and summarise what has been discussed. Lastly they will need to use silence actively.

The interviewer also needs to communicate that they are listening. This will be done most effectively through the way they behave:

- Maintain an open, attentive posture.
- Maintain eye contact without staring in a disconcerting way.

- Give an indication that you are listening by, for example, nodding or leaning forward.
- Do not interrupt.
- Do not fire unconnected questions.
- Do not change the subject without summarising what has been said and agreed, and checking whether there is anything the person being interviewed wants to add.

Active silence

When people are talking they should be allowed to take their time. The interviewer should not be put off by silence. They should consider what is going on in the silence: is it an active silence? Is the person being interviewed using the silence to think, or are they waiting for the interviewer to say something? If they are thinking, not being interrupted will help them. Interruptions which are too hasty might distract them. Some people, however, may need prompting if they are stuck, for example:

'Did anything else happen?'

'What happened after they shouted at your kids?'

'Is there anything else you want to tell me?'

Pace of the interview

People being interviewed should be allowed to finish what they are saying. If the interviewer is not sure whether they have finished, the person being interviewed should be asked before continuing with the next question.

Interviewers should not just plunge on regardless at the first break in the conversation. The key to a successful interview is to give it the time it needs, without hurrying or unnecessarily protracting it.

Pace is a matter of judgement, but the interviewer should check with the person being interviewed that the pace is right for them. If people are distressed or upset, there will obviously be a need to take the interview more slowly. The pace of the interview should not be decided by the interviewer's attention span, diary or workload.

Verbal and non-verbal messages

People being interviewed will respond not only to what is said but also to the way in which it is said. The physical cues used to discern whether people mean what they say, and the extent of their sincerity, include eye contact, facial expression, tone and volume of voice, body position and gestures. So-called body language or non-verbal communication can either add power and force to, or it can detract from, contradict or minimise, what is said.

Verbal and non-verbal messages must be congruent. Where they are not, the listener becomes confused and either disbelieves entirely what is being said, or interprets it through their own feelings. For example, if the interviewer says 'we will do everything we can to help,' without looking at the person, or in a very soft voice, the tenant, who may already be feeling distressed and uncertain, will understand that statement to mean 'we will try, but there is likely to be little that we can actually do'. If that same statement is made in a tone that is peremptory and abrupt, by an interviewer staring directly in a challenging way at the person being interviewed, the statement will be taken to mean 'we have to say we will help, but we won't do much because we are not taking your complaint seriously'.

If, however, that statement is made in a calm, clearly audible voice, with the interviewer maintaining direct eye contact and giving congruent behavioural messages by, for example, leaning forward or nodding, the person being interviewed is likely to feel a degree of confidence that the interviewer will indeed do what they can to help and, perhaps more importantly, that what they do *will* in fact help.

Everyone has their own behavioural norms and habits. To those that know them well, the message of what they say is not misunderstood; however to strangers everyday or habitual behaviour, such as looking away when talking to someone or arms folded across the chest, may detract from or contradict what is being said.

To ensure the message is received and understood as intended, and not disbelieved or misinterpreted, here are some questions about behaviour or body language the interviewer should ask themself.

Eye contact
Do I look another person directly in the eye when I am talking to them? Do my eyes shift away when talking? Do I lower my eyes when I am feeling doubtful, uncertain or negative? Do I stare in a way that makes people uncomfortable, or turn away feeling intimidated or unsure of themselves?

Facial expression
Do I smile at inappropriate moments, more out of anxiety, and not because I am amused in any way? Do I look severe and unfriendly, when I really am just feeling serious? Is the fact that I am listening clearly communicated through my behaviour – do I nod, or make a sound of acknowledgement? Do I look bored? Do I look inappropriately anxious?

Voice tone and volume
Do I find it difficult to use a firm tone of voice? How do I behave when I am interrupted? Do I press on regardless, or do I stop and listen to what they are saying? If it is important that I finish what I was saying, do I say that, then ensure they are listening before continuing? Can people I am speaking to hear me clearly? Do I appeal to others in a child-like voice? Do I speak too loudly or too slowly to someone whose first language is not the same as mine?

Body position and gestures
Do I generally stand or sit too near or too far from the other person? (A good indication of this is if the other person moves away, or leans back.) Do I wring my hands, fiddle with my hair, jewellery or pen, fidget, doodle etc.? Do I sit forward in my chair when I am anxious? Do I lean forward when I am trying to emphasise a point? Do I lean back and slouch looking indifferent when I really am listening? Do I sit with my arms folded across my chest looking defensive and excluding? Does the position

of my arms, by my side or on my knees, convey openness and interest?

Seeking advice on body language

It is unlikely that any individual knows straightaway the answer to every one of the questions above. Most people have some insight into how they appear to others. However, to find out in detail about the above areas, interviewers are advised to ask someone who knows them well, and whom they can trust to be honest with them, for their feedback, not only about their current body language but also what they might do differently to get their message across more effectively.

Questioning

The interviewer should ask questions one at a time. Asking double-headed or multiple questions is not likely to be successful because the person being interviewed will forget some of the questions and answer only the ones that they remember. The interviewer will therefore not get a clear picture.

Open questions

Open questions provide a framework for the respondent in terms of subject matter, but they impose no constraints on the time a person takes to answer or the information they volunteer in answering the question. Open questions do not pre-suppose a particular answer, nor do they restrict the answer to Yes or No.

These are examples of open questions:

'Can you tell me as much as you can remember about the incident that took place?'

'Can you describe the person who attacked you in as much detail as you can remember?'

Rephrasing open questions

Interviewers on occasion need to rephrase their questions, either because the person being interviewed has misunderstood, or because the question was not clear first time. There is then a temptation to follow an open question with a leading question such as: 'Were the people who did it young white boys then?' Interviewers should therefore have ready a rephrasing of their original question which is as open as the first variant. So, if the original question was: 'Have there been any other incidents other than the one outside the school?', another way of phrasing the question would be: 'Has anything happened involving the same people at your house or in the street or anywhere else?'

Follow-up questions

Once the person being interviewed has been given the time to answer the open question as fully as they can, the interviewer may need to ask follow-up or probing questions.

Interviewers should not interject with follow-up questions while the person being interviewed is answering the original open question. They should allow them to finish, and as they are speaking make notes about the follow-up questions they want to ask. Once the person has finished, the follow-up questions can be put one at a time.

There are two sorts of follow-up questions: ones which clarify a previous answer, seek more detail or make sure the interviewer has fully understood what is being said; and ones which move the interview on to a new subject.

The first type may well be a fact-seeking closed question (see page 91). Examples of follow-up questions of this sort are:

'Could you confirm the number of people involved?'

'Have there been similar incidents on other occasions?'

However, it is helpful to summarise the first answer before asking another question, so questions might be better phrased as in these examples:

'You said that it was local kids who shouted abuse at your children. Do you know who they were?'

Or

'You mentioned that it was kids who were throwing stones through your windows and shouting abuse. Had you seen them before at all?'

The second type of follow-up question that moves the person being interviewed onto a new subject is, for example:

'This incident happened outside your home. Has anything like this ever happened anywhere else?'

Focusing on the incidents as recounted by the person harassed is far more effective than facing them with a barrage of questions. This latter approach suggests that the interviewer has not really been listening. It also suggests that they are rather indifferent to how upset the person experiencing harassment is feeling. Focusing further questions around the answer to the initial open question encourages the person being interviewed to believe they are being listened to and taken seriously. They will therefore feel more confident about opening up and giving a full account.

This approach of prefacing a question with a summary of previous answers gives continuity to the interview and again confirms to the person being interviewed that the interviewer is paying close attention to what they are saying.

Closed questions
Closed questions seek factual information. They are appropriate only for that purpose. They do not encourage the person being interviewed to open up or to give a full account of what has taken place. Examples of closed questions are:

'Where did the incident you told me about take place?'
'What time of day was it when this happened?'
'Did anyone see what happened?'

Leading questions

Leading questions imply the answer in the way the question is phrased. They usually require the answer Yes or No. It is appropriate to use leading questions in interviews of people experiencing harassment only as a means of clarification, or as a prelude to summarising and reflecting (see page 93).

The obvious danger of leading questions is that they put words into the mouth of the person being interviewed, and may therefore sustain or continue a misunderstanding on the interviewer's part, because the person being interviewed lacks the self-confidence or assertiveness to contradict. Examples of leading questions are:

'So you would agree that...?'

'Was that because...?'

Loaded questions

Loaded questions contain a value judgement in the way they are phrased which often undermines the objectivity of the interviewer's question. Examples of loaded questions are:

'Couldn't you have shouted back at them?'

'Why didn't you call the police straightaway?'

'Did you do anything to upset them?'

'Isn't it just kids messing around?'

Questions such as these are not appropriate for interviews of people who have experienced harassment because they can convey disbelief, suspicion or aggression.

Summarising and reflecting

Interviews with people experiencing racial harassment are often long and complicated. Too often discussions move too quickly to the possibility of being transferred to another property or some other drastic action that might be taken before all the information has been gathered and the options discussed.

To prevent this, the interview should be conducted in measured stages (see chapter 7). There is a technique to summarising and reflecting back on what has been agreed which brings one section of the interview to an end and forms a bridge into the next section. The person being interviewed then knows exactly where they are in the interview. It is an opportunity to ensure that all relevant information has been provided, and that the interviewer has a complete, accurate record in their notes.

The interviewee knows that what they have said has been heard and understood and will be acted on. They will also be reassured that they will not have to repeat anything they have already said when moving on to the next stage. Thus they can focus on the questions that are being asked in the next stage without worrying that they have not made the points they want to make sufficiently strongly in response to the questions already asked. For example:

'Before we move on to discuss what we can do to stop these incidents, can I just summarise what we have agreed that we can do to improve the security of your home?

We are going to put safety glass in the outside windows and install a fireproof metal letter box and a security light outside the front door.

Is there anything else we can do that you think would make the place feel more safe?'

In summarising, it is often useful for the interviewer to repeat the reasons people give for feeling the way they do. This reinforces the impression that the interviewer is taking in what has disturbed the person being harassed:

'You said it was when those boys began shouting that you felt frightened...do you happen to know where any of them live?'

Use of interpreters

Many people who experience harassment do not speak English as a first language. Some also use sign language as their first language. The responsibility for arranging interpretation facilities rests with the interviewer and their organisation, not with the person being interviewed. It goes without saying that a primary success factor for the interviewer is having clear two-way communication.

Adopting an approach which is designed to empower the person being harassed to seek help and to help themself is hardly likely to be facilitated by a struggle to communicate. The implied message may be 'I am leaving you to struggle through this interview,' further implying that, 'If I am not willing to help you here and now, it is hardly credible that I will be able to do anything to stop the unacceptable behaviour'.

Even where the person being interviewed can in the interviewer's opinion communicate sufficiently well in English, they should always be asked before the interview starts in which language they feel that they can communicate and understand best; if this is not English an interpreter should be arranged.

In most instances, interpretation or translation is best done by professionals who understand both the language in question and the subject under discussion. It is to be hoped that such people will be amongst the organisation's staff, although this clearly cannot always be guaranteed.

Using staff as interpreters puts an extra burden upon them, above doing the job for which they are paid. It is also not appropriate to use them when the subject under discussion is confidential. There should therefore be access in all organisations to professional interpreters, if necessary through an agency. Interpreters should also be briefed and, if necessary, trained before assisting at interviews. They need clear, technical briefing – for example on matters of law.

There are also facilities and agencies widely available for

interpretation on the telephone and translation and print-ing of written material. However, interpretation over the phone should be seen only as a desperate last resort, as an interview conducted in this way would undermine almost all the points of good practice that this chapter has spelt out.

Children should never be used as interpreters in inter-views about harassment, or for that matter any other com-plex or confidential matter.

In many instances relatives and friends are used as inter-preters. Whilst there may be no problem with this on day-to-day matters, it is not appropriate for matters which are confidential or stressful such as harassment, rent arrears or other financial matters, health, personal care and so on. There is however a possibility that someone who has been harassed may be more comfortable in the reassuring pres-ence of a familiar, supportive relative or friend. They should be asked to interpret only if the person being harassed finds the presence of a professional interpreter off-putting or intimidating.

Relatives and friends may also have their own views about the right course of action for the person attacked and so may not always be impartial and objective. Again the person being harassed is not empowered if infor-mation is withheld, filtered or misrepresented through someone else's opinion. The relative may be acting more like an advocate, how ever well-meaning, rather than as an interpreter.

The person being interviewed should be asked whether they want a relative, friend or neighbour to interpret, or whether they want an independent interpreter, or whether in some cases they might be happy with both the relative and the interpreter present. This last option is worth offering, as people may genuinely want an independent interpreter but be afraid to say so for fear of offending friends and relatives. In any case, the choice should be theirs.

Staff or volunteers from community groups are also called upon to act as interpreters. There are a number of problems with this: they are not always readily available; they are providing a service for which they are not being paid; and they may have their own legitimate campaigning concerns which may not make their interpretation accurate or objective.

Technical jargon is also complicated, hard enough to understand if you speak excellent English. If the interpreter has little grasp of the concepts, and the tenant even less, the opportunities for misunderstanding are considerable. Interpreters therefore need to be briefed on the concepts, the organisation's internal systems, and the systems and approaches of relevant outside agencies before they begin interpreting. Where an interpreter is used on a regular basis, they should receive training in those areas from housing management staff.

Note-taking

The interviewer needs to explain that they will have to take notes during the interview and that these notes will be to help them remember the discussion, and to make a complete, accurate record. They will not be used to disclose information to anyone outside, even within the organisation. The record will be shown only to identified individuals you told the interviewee about in your comments about confidentiality.

It is obviously important that accurate records are kept of discussions, both with people experiencing racial harassment and with perpetrators. Much emphasis has been laid on ensuring that the interviewer's behaviour communicates empathy and support for the people experiencing racial harassment. An inappropriate approach to taking notes may significantly undermine the views of the person harassed about the interviewer's commitment to supporting them.

If the person being interviewed feels that the notes are being kept in order that they could be challenged in the future, or to ensure that they do not change their mind or are held accountable for what they have said, they will be reluctant to be open and frank. They may not therefore provide as full an account as the interviewer would like. The interviewer's insensitive approach may add to their sense of being harassed, not only by the perpetrator, but also by the interviewer.

At the beginning of the interview the interviewer should make it clear first that they need to take notes and secondly what use those notes will be put to. For example, in explaining how the interview is going to be conducted the interviewer could say something like:

'It's important to get a full and accurate account of what's happened so we can make sure we give you all the support that you need. We also might just need the information to take action against the person who attacked you. So, if it's all right, I'm going to take some notes to make sure we have a good record of the case. If we keep good records, it makes it easier for us to help you do what you think is best.

I'll read through what I've written at the end so you can be sure I've got it all down accurately. Is that all right with you?'

Interviewers should record as closely as possible what people actually say, not adding their own interpretation. The purpose of keeping the notes is accuracy, not to make judgements. Interviewers are therefore advised to write out the key questions in advance. They can, if they use the suggested proforma (see page 148), write the answers as they receive them.

Notes can be read back at the end of each stage in the interview to help summarise. Once the interviewer has got confirmation of the notes' accuracy, they should ask the person being interviewed whether they have anything more to add which should be included.

CHAPTER 7

THE FIRST VISIT

Who should conduct the interview? /
Location / Objectives / Structure / Key stages /
*Introductions / Ground rules / Finding out
what happened / Explaining the organisation's
policy / Generating options for action / Ensuring
safety in and around the home / Discussing action
against perpetrators / Discussing transfers /
Financial support / Next steps for the person being
harassed / Next steps for the organisation / Ending
the interview* / Following up the interview

Who should conduct the interview?

Continuity is important in ensuring that someone who is being harassed or attacked feels supported. Ideally the person conducting the first interview should be the person responsible for handling the case thereafter.

If the incident is reported to the landlord, the best person to carry out the interview is the housing manager on whose patch the tenant lives. There may, however, be some circumstances when this is not appropriate. If the last contact between the housing manager and the tenant was threatening action for rent arrears or serving notice of seeking possession, the person being harassed is unlikely fully to trust that housing manager's commitment to assist them. Their scepticism may be unfounded, but it is nonetheless real. On the other hand the housing manager may indeed, as a result of previous contact, or just prejudice, be less than willing to help the tenant.

Research by Brunel University indicates that the effectiveness with which reports of racial incidents are handled is in part dependent on the previous relationship between the interviewer and the person being interviewed. So, for example, a landlord's previous failure to complete repairs is likely to undermine the tenant's confidence that something will be done if they do report the incident. They may then not report the incident at all, or be less than frank because of their scepticism.

If these circumstances apply to the person who would normally have primary casework responsibility, the case should be handled by another staff member.

It may be the case that the person who has been harassed would prefer to be interviewed by someone who speaks their language, someone of their own race, or a woman. This is, of course, their right, and they should be offered this specific option if it is available, even if that is not the housing manager normally responsible for the estate, the patch or the area.

An organisation receiving a report of racial harassment, whether it is the police or the landlord, may have specialist staff dealing with racial attacks or harassment.

Individual authorities and police forces have their own procedural guidance. However, given the number of potential racial incidents, it is difficult to imagine that any has enough specialist staff to deal with every incident. In general, therefore, the first visit is still best conducted by the caseworker for the patch, either the housing manager or the beat or duty police officer. If at the first interview the case seems complicated or requires a specialist input, it may then be appropriate for further work on the case to be undertaken by specialist staff.

A case may also require an early input from a manager. Again this depends on its complexity or severity. Before the first interview, it is possible that the principal caseworker may not be able to handle the case, perhaps because of inexperience. Then the line manager would do well to attend that interview, even if the primary responsibility for the case remains with the caseworker, both during the interview and thereafter.

Location

Once an incident has been reported, the first interview needs to take place as soon as possible afterwards. If the report is taken in person by the housing manager who will be dealing with the case, it might be appropriate to conduct the interview immediately in the office. A quiet, private space such as an interview room is needed, where the interview can take place without interruption.

If the report is taken on the telephone by any other

member of staff, an appointment should be made for the person attacked to be interviewed, ideally within 24 hours. They should be asked where they would prefer the interview to be conducted. They are likely to feel more at ease in their own home. It also does not put them to the inconvenience of making a visit to the office.

Interviews conducted in the home give the interviewer a much better sense of the incidents that have taken place, particularly if they are not familiar with the property, the street or the area. A home visit is a concrete demonstration that the housing manager is prepared to go out to people who have been attacked. It can in itself be seen as a sign of support. Then psychologically, any support offered within the home is likely to carry more weight with the tenant than anything that is said in the office environment. From all of these perspectives, the home is probably the best place for the interview.

Objectives

The most important objective of the first visit is not to gain information, or to investigate. It is to reassure and offer support and to identify what practical and emotional support the tenant may need. Secondly, the interviewer will want to convey to the tenant that they individually will offer all the help they can, and that the organisation is committed to supporting people experiencing harassment. Only after these messages have been clearly conveyed should the process of gathering information begin.

The last objective of the visit is to decide on next steps.

Structure

The interview should be clearly structured with these objectives in mind. Without a structure, interviewers will find that they depart lacking information they need. In some cases this will also leave the tenant feeling confused and uncertain about what is going to happen next. They may feel ignored because nothing is going to be done quickly enough, or at all, to assist and support them. They may be left with a sense of fear — of going out, of further incidents or of reprisals resulting from insensitive or indiscreet action by the authorities. They may even be concerned that the housing officer will inadvertently reveal their identity to the perpetrators or their allies.

Perhaps the worst possible outcome is that the original attack is compounded by a further onslaught from the housing officer in the interview — a barrage of difficult, unanswerable questions such as:

'Who did it?'

'What was their racial origin?'

'Do you know where they live?'

'Have you contacted the police?'

'Do you want us to go round and see them?'

If the answer to any of these questions is 'I don't know', or 'No', then the feeling of powerlessness that is likely to have been experienced at the time of the attack or harassment will be made greater by the sense that nothing can be, or is going to be, done or that reporting incidents only leads to a complex, unhelpful interview and no action to stop the harassment.

Key stages

The key stages in the interview are:

1. Introductions.
2. Agreeing ground rules for the interview, for example, on confidentiality, on action only by consent of the person attacked, on the role of relatives, interpreters, children or anyone else present, and on the arrangements for note-taking.
3. Finding out what happened:
   - the incident itself
   - where it occurred
   - when it occurred
   - were the perpetrators known and identified?
   - were there any witnesses?
4. Explaining the organisation's policy to seek to stop harassment by:
   - a commitment to preventing harassment
   - practical and emotional support for people experiencing harassment
   - taking action where possible against perpetrators.

5. Offering reassurance, empathy and support, particularly ensuring the physical safety of the person who has been harassed and their family.
6. Identifying sources of practical support.
7. Possible action against the perpetrator by:
    • the landlord
    • other agencies, such as the police
    • the tenant themself.
8. Next steps for the person being harassed.
9. Next steps for the interviewer and the organisation they represent.
10. Ending the interview.

Introductions

To begin with the interviewer should introduce themself and anyone who is with them such as an interpreter or a colleague. They should also ask the people being interviewed to introduce themselves and any relatives and children who are present. The interviewer will want to know all their names.

Ground rules

Children present

If possible, children should not be present at the interview. They might inhibit the person being interviewed, who may not want to upset or distress them, and they may become upset by what they hear. They may also interrupt or disrupt the interview. The interviewer should therefore suggest that they go to another room.

If, however, this is likely to cause distress or upset either to the parents or the children, the interview should continue with them present. If the interview is taking place in the office parents should be asked if they would mind the children being looked after by another member of staff, with toys, in another room.

Confidentiality

The interviewer should stress what the arrangements are for confidentiality and anonymity. It is not possible or appropriate to guarantee absolute confidentiality – in the sense of not discussing the case with anybody else. The case will, for example, have to be discussed with the interviewer's line manager and may, if the harassment persists, have to be referred to a racial harassment panel or working party, which may involve people from other agencies.

The interviewer should be explicit and clear about who else will be informed about the case, and give an absolute assurance that the perpetrator, other tenants, or other agencies will not be informed without the interviewee's explicit consent. Even if consent is given to a warning visit to the perpetrator, they should be reassured that anonymity will be respected. The perpetrator will not be informed, even if they ask, who reported the case.

Consent

At an early stage in the interview it is important to confirm to the person attacked that nothing will be done without their consent. They will be kept informed once action has been taken, and their consent sought before further action is taken.

Finding out what happened

Only once a clear framework for the interview has been explained can the information gathering process begin. The interviewer will want as full an account as they can get from the person of exactly what took place, where it happened, at what time, who was involved, and if anyone else saw the incident.

The interviewers should seek to gain each of these pieces of information in turn. It is best to start by asking an open question such as: 'Could you tell me exactly what happened? It would be helpful if you could include as many details as you can remember.' Once the person has answered that question the interviewer can follow it up with prompts based on the questions listed above, using the techniques outlined in chapter 6.

Explaining the organisation's policy

Once the interviewer has found out what took place they should explain the policy of their organisation.

An effective policy in a school, housing organisation or for the police will state clearly the organisation's condemnation of intentional, unprovoked, targeted attacks or harassment and will have the following objectives:

1. to stop the harassment and attacks
2. to support the person being harassed – practically and emotionally
3. if the harassment persists, to take action against the perpetrators.

The interviewer should explain this to reassure the person

harassed. The interviewer should then confirm that they understand fully that the organisation wishes to support them and will only do what is in their best interest, as they define it, and will take whatever action is necessary.

Generating options for action

As the first interview's principal purpose is to empower the person experiencing harassment about what action can be taken to support them, by what agencies and in what ways, the interviewer's job is to generate options and thereby give the person harassed a choice about the next steps that are going to be taken. It is not the interviewer's job either to tell the person harassed what is in their best interest, or that what they want to happen is impossible.

Whilst the interviewer might be trying to be helpful by giving a realistic assessment of how possible their desired course of action is, or suggesting alternatives to them that they have not suggested themself, the interviewer should bear in mind that removing choice and control over the next steps effectively disempowers that person and reinforces their status as a victim not only of harassment, but also of over-rigid bureaucratic decision-making. Thus the attempt to support and help can become part of the problem, not part of the solution.

The interviewer will inevitably focus on the sanctions with which they are most familiar. This will invariably mean landlord and tenant matters for housing organisations' representatives. For schools, the focus may be on the possibility of excluding the perpetrators temporarily from school, although this may result in the same young people harassing other people on the street or in their homes. For the police the focus may be on the likely success of criminal action, taking into account the need to collect convincing evidence sufficient to satisfy both the Crown Prosecution Service and the courts. As most crimes committed are never considered by a court, police officers will inevitably retain a degree of scepticism about the viability of criminal action.

Indeed much emphasis in the past has been given either to taking action against the perpetrators – particularly repossession proceedings by the landlord – or to transfer-ring people who have been harassed. Before housing managers focus exclusively on those specific aspects of landlord and tenant matters they should first work through with the person who has been harassed what sup-port agencies there are available. This might include the police, schools and education authorities, local authority social services departments, citizens' advice bureaux, law centres, victim support schemes, community agencies, advocates or landlords.

Once the person experiencing harassment knows that there are a number of different sources of support available they may be able to think more clearly about the fact that they do have options and choices. The interviewer can then work through with the person harassed what action these different agencies might take, including of course the interviewer's own organisation.

Ensuring safety in and around the home

An immediate area to consider is the household. The interviewer will first want to detail the arrangements for carrying out emergency repairs, such as fixing locks on doors, boarding up or reglazing windows, removing graffiti and so on. In addition, they may suggest a visit from someone who could inspect the home and consider ways of improving security – at the landlord's expense. Further options for practical support which the interview should explore are detailed in chapter 8.

Discussing action against perpetrators

Only once the safety of both the building and the person have been secured will it be appropriate to go on to talk about what other steps could be taken, for example action against perpetrators. Clearly the interviewer has first to establish whether the perpetrator was seen and, if so, identified. Sometimes a person experiencing harassment will say that the perpetrators are not known to them, when they may be. They are keen to avoid reprisals against them or their family and therefore they think it is wiser 'not to rock the boat'. The interviewer needs to reassure the interviewee that they will speak to the perpetrators only with their consent and only if they agree it is in their best interests.

Don't say	'Can you tell us who did it so that we can go round and see them?'
Do say	'It would be helpful if we knew who had been involved, although we will not go round and see them without your consent. Were you able to identify them?'
	'Did you see who was involved?'

If the perpetrators have been identified, but the person attacked has reservations about the interviewer visiting them, they should be offered some reassurances about the purpose of the visit to the perpetrator, how it would be handled, that their anonymity could be maintained if they wished, and that they would be supported if the perpetrator continued to harass them after the visit. If they are still reluctant, they should not be forced, but it may be possible to return to the subject on a subsequent visit.[50]

Don't say	'Unless we know who did it, we can't do anything about it.'
	'Of course if we do go and see them, that might make it worse.'
Do say	'If we do go to see them, we will make sure you are happy with us doing that first. Also, we won't tell them who reported the incidents if you don't want us to.'
	'Are you worried that our visit might cause further problems?'
	'We will try to make sure it doesn't. We'll want to warn them that what they've been doing could be a breach of the tenancy agreement, and if they go on they might lose their home or the police could take action against them.'

[50]This is covered in more detail in Lemos G (1993), *Interviewing Perpetrators of Racial Harassment: a guide for housing managers*, Lemos & Crane.

> 'We'll make it clear that if they do anything else, they'll get reported and we'll take action against them for breaking the tenancy agreement.'
>
> 'At this stage, you won't have to give evidence or anything.'

Action against perpetrators need not be specific. It might, for example, involve a general letter to all tenants in the neighbourhood warning them that racial harassment is a breach of their tenancy agreement and may result in them losing their home.

The focus of the discussion about any further action should be: how is the unacceptable behaviour to be stopped? People who have been attacked are rarely seeking revenge or punishment. They are generally more interested in being able to live in their home in peace.

Warnings such as the general letter mentioned above are one possible way to achieve this. There may be others, for example, by contacting a school or asking the police to contact the family. The options for police action are discussed in chapter 2.

More generally, action against perpetrators is discussed in detail in the companion volumes to this one.[51]

---

[51] Lemos G (1993), *Interviewing Perpetrators of Racial Harassment – a guide for housing managers*, Lemos & Crane and Seager R and Jeffries J (1994), *Eliminating Racial Harassment – a guide to policies and procedures*, Lemos & Crane.

Discussing transfers

Only if personal security and security of buildings cannot be secured and nothing can be done to deter or stop the attacks or harassment, should the possibility of the person experiencing harassment being transferred to another property be considered. There may be no alternative to this either because the person involved is so frightened and requires something be done immediately, or because the perpetrators are unidentified and there is no way of identifying them quickly. It may also be that the move is temporary while action is taken against the perpetrator, and until it is safe for the person who has been attacked to move back.

Financial support

The interviewer also needs to tell the person harassed and who is considering moving, what help is available with the move. Does the landlord pay for removal or home loss costs? Do they make a contribution to redecoration expenditure? Should the person attacked be compensated? Have any other costs been incurred, or are any likely to be incurred, which the person attacked might need help with?

Next steps for the person being harassed

The interviewer will want to agree both on what the interviewer's organisation will to do next and on what the person attacked is going to do as a result of the interview. Chapter 6 discusses empowerment. Focusing exclusively on the actions of the interviewer's organisation denies the person attacked any control, power or perhaps even influence over the outcome.

Some possible actions that the person harassed could take would include:

- to contact other support agencies. The interviewer could leave them a list of names and telephone numbers.
- to record further incidents accurately.
- to report further incidents to the landlord, the police, the social services or education authorities.
- to organise a network of personal support, for example, escorting children to school or to the shops.

Discussing diary sheets and records of attacks

Far too many potential criminal and civil actions against perpetrators of harassment have either not been prosecuted, or have not been sustained in court because of the poor quality of recording of the incidents which occur. Lawyers are left with little ammunition for successful action.

However, people being harassed can experience the need to keep records as another form of harassment. The retaining of evidence, such as hate mail, or not clearing up rubbish that has been deliberately dumped outside their house can be irksome and depressing. In addition, these incidents have to be recorded on a semi-official form, the logging of which is no pleasure to anyone, but without which the person harassed may well have been informed no action is possible.

The interviewer should therefore clearly explain both the need for accurate records in a non-intimidating way; and how the records should be kept, the information sought and the level of detail required. Information is needed not only about what happened, when and where, but also about the nature of the perpetrator, particularly as one of the perennial problems in dealing with harassment is the fact that perpetrators are either not seen or, if they are seen, not identified.

A tape recorder or a camera can also be helpful in recording what happened as described by the person attacked if they are not comfortable with filling in forms, for reasons of literacy, or because English is not their first language, or for some other reason.

The following information is needed about the incidents themselves:

• Where did they take place?
• What happened, described as fully as possible?
• Exactly what time?
• Did anyone else see what happened?
• Who were the witnesses, and where do they live?
• Were the perpetrators seen, known or identified?

The Metropolitan Police have issued guidance to people who are being attacked about what information they find helpful in identifying suspected perpetrators. This includes getting details of the suspect's sex, height, age and build as well as features such as skin, eye and hair colour, the shape of their face and mouth, as well as distinguishing features such as hairstyle, clothing and marks or scars.[52]

Next steps for the organisation
The interviewer will also want to summarise for the

[52] *Racial Harassment Action Guide* (1989), Metropolitan Police.

person they are interviewing what the next steps they are going to take will be. These may include:

- taking agreed practical action, for example improving security, or arranging a visit from the crime prevention officer
- visiting and interviewing the perpetrator
- ensuring that all incidents that have taken place so far are properly recorded
- contacting other agencies, for example, out-of-hours helplines
- agreeing time and place for follow-up visits.

Ending the interview

The interview should be ended when the person being interviewed is ready to end it, not when the interviewer wants to, or feels they have gone as far as they can or has a time deadline to meet.

The interviewer should make sure that the person being interviewed has nothing to add to what has already been discussed. Then they should ask whether they agree with the notes that have been taken, and if they would be willing to sign them as an accurate record of the interview.

It is also helpful to agree a time and a place to meet again for a follow-up visit. The content of these visits is discussed in chapter 9. Before leaving, the interviewer should reassure the person attacked that they are available, and where and when they can be contacted, if they have anything else they want to discuss or report.

Following up the interview

It is good practice to write to the person interviewed confirming the discussion, any decisions that were taken and any progress made subsequently. This should obviously be done in a language that is appropriate.

CHAPTER 8

PRACTICAL SUPPORT

Providing information / A secure environment /
A security package / Specialist staff / Self-help
groups / Emergency helplines / Advocacy /
Working with other agencies / Getting the
police involved / Rehousing / *Rehousing options* /
Reletting / *Financial assistance*

There are many different aspects to practical support that
can be offered, ranging from the provision of information,
to the security of buildings and the safety of people, transfers, financial assistance, and advocacy and counselling.
All of these are discussed below.

Providing information

Circle 33 Housing Trust provide all those who have been
harassed with an information pack as follows[53]:

---

[53] *Tenant Support Pack* Circle 33 Housing Trust.

Tenant Support Pack

Introduction
The Trust condemns harassment and takes all reports seriously. This pack provides you with a summary of our policy and tells you what you can expect from us if you report harassment. It also contains an Incident Report form for you to fill in, details of the legal options available and a list of other agencies that may be able to provide help and support.

We hope this pack outlines clearly what we can do. Our main aim is to stop harassment. Your housing officer will be your main contact so speak to them if you need any more information on our harassment policy or how we can help.

While we hope and try to be effective in tackling harassment we have to acknowledge that there are limits to what we can do. We cannot always deal with harassment as effectively as we or you would like. In particular where there is persistent and organised harassment in an area we will need the co-operation of other agencies such as the Police or local authority in dealing with the problem. We can help you get in touch with other agencies. Where we wish to take legal action we will need witnesses and evidence to support our case in court. If the person harassing you is not our tenant we have fewer sanctions.

Tenant Information Leaflet: Harassment[54]

What is harassment

Harassment is any deliberate attack suffered by an individual or group because of their ethnic origin, sex, sexual preference, HIV/AIDS status, age, mental health problem or disability where the recipient believes and/or there is evidence that the perpetrator was acting on these grounds.

Ethnic origin includes colour, race, religion, national or ethnic origin.

The Trust also recognises that some people are harassed without there being any element of prejudice or discrimination.

What you can expect from Circle 33 if you report harassment

First steps

The first thing we will do is arrange to talk to you, preferably in your own home, about the incident/s. Our aim is for this interview to take place within 2 working days of you reporting the incident. Your housing officer will try to find out more about what has happened. If you give consent he or she will approach the alleged perpetrator about the incident/s and explain the Trust's policy on dealing with harassment. He or she will be warned of the consequences of harassment. Also, if you give consent your housing officer will speak to any other witness/es to get more evidence.

---

[54] *Tenants Handbook* Circle 33 Housing Trust.

This investigation will take about 5 working days. A meeting will then be held where a team of housing officers, team leader and area manager will decide what action will be taken to deal with the harassment. In some cases the Trust may decide that harassment has not occurred and will decide on a different approach to the problem. Your housing officer will write to you or visit you within 3 days of the meeting and let you know what has been decided.

There may be some situations where we will have to take quicker action, for example where your life is in danger.

Deciding on a course of action
What we will do will partially depend on what you want. But we will not always be able to do everything you want us to do. Even after investigation it is sometimes difficult to be clear exactly what is happening. The action we take will depend on:

- How serious the attack/s have been
- How the harassment is affecting you
- How effective we think a course of action will be. (There's no point going to court if we know we won't win)
- What evidence is available
- The resources available

The action we can take to support you may include:

- Providing additional security to your home so you feel safer in it, e.g. security grilles
- Trying to find alternative accommodation with the council or another housing association
- Putting you in touch with other agencies that can provide you with advice and support

- Offering you a transfer. This is only possible in the most serious cases where there have been physical assaults or a life endangering incident, or because of the harassment you are no longer able to live in your home. Although we will do our utmost, we will not always be able to offer people the transfer they want, when they want.

The action we can take to deal with the perpetrator may include:
- Visiting and sending warning letters to the perpetrator. Sometimes this action alone will stop the harassment.
- Taking legal action against the perpetrator. It is possible to take out injunctions to stop harassment. We can also take a tenant who is causing harassment to court to repossess their home. To be successful we need evidence and witnesses and this is why it is important you complete incident report forms and let us contact other witnesses.

What we would like you to do
Your housing officer will keep in touch with you to keep you informed about what we are doing. He or she will agree with you how often you will be visited. If other incidents occur please fill in incident report form, enclosed, to keep a record of further incidents. This will help us take effective action against the perpetrator.

We encourage you to report incidents to the Police who can take action against perpetrators of harassment.

Appeals

If you are not happy with the decisions made and the action taken you can appeal using the Trusts complaint procedure. A separate leaflet and form is available from your area office.

Legal options

In cases of harassment various legal actions can be taken. The following is a very brief guide to how the law can be used. Three forms of action are explained – possession proceedings, injunctions and criminal proceedings. In possession cases it is up to the landlord to take action. Either the tenant or, in some cases the landlord can apply for injunctions. The Police can also take action under various laws. It will always be important to have evidence and witnesses so your co-operation is vital.

Possession proceedings

Harassment is a breach of the tenancy agreement and will usually also constitute nuisance, which is also a breach of the tenancy agreement. Where Circle 33 can prove harassment has taken place it is possible to issue proceedings and ultimately repossess the property. Proving harassment has taken place will depend on having witnesses and evidence.

Your housing officer will explain in more detail the steps we have to take to seek possession of a property. In summary, there are four main stages:

1. We have to serve notice on the tenant
2. We have to apply to court for a hearing
3. We have to go to court to have an order granted
4. We have to seek a warrant for eviction

It can be a lengthy process.

Taking successful legal action in harassment cases is difficult but possible.

A case is more likely to be successful if the harassment:
- has continued for a period of time
- is serious and deliberate

and if we have lots of evidence and witnesses.

Injunctions

Injunctions can be a quick, if temporary solution. Witnesses may have to appear in court. There are three types of injunction:
- Perpetual

To permanently stop the perpetrator from carrying out harassment
- Interlocutory

To temporarily stop the harassment, until for example trial for possession is held
- Quia timet

To prevent threatened harassment

'Ex parte' injunctions can be used in emergencies. The defendant is not given notice and witnesses may not have to appear. In court, affidavits are needed. These injunctions may only last a few days.

Failure to comply with an injunction can result in a fine or imprisonment. In practice injunctions can take time to enforce as there is no power of arrest attached and no immediate action can be taken if the injunction is broken.[54A]

Injunctions can be sought either by the person suffering the nuisance or by the landlord where the tenant is in breach of the tenancy agreement, or by the landlord to

[54A]The Housing Act 1996 now gives judges the discretion to add the power of arrest to the provisions of an injunction granted in the High Court or county court.

prevent a tenant causing permanent damage to their property.

It is possible on an application for an injunction the court at its own discretion may seek an undertaking from the defendant to stop particular behaviour. This is similar to an injunction and may mean witnesses do not have to appear in court.

Combination of injunction and possession

An injunction can be sought pending possession proceedings, protecting tenants until possession proceedings take place. Breach of an injunction or undertaking can strengthen the case for possession. If an injunction is successful the court is unlikely to grant possession as the problem will have ceased.

Criminal proceedings

In cases of harassment the police can take criminal proceedings against the harasser. The following is some of the legislation that can be used:

Criminal Law Offences Against the Person Act 1861

In cases of common assault (causing a reasonable person to fear an attack), assault and battery (where physical contact occurs) and assault with actual bodily harm.

Public Order Act 1986

In cases of affray (using or threatening violence), incitement to racial hatred (using threatening words or behaviour).

Protection from Eviction Act 1977
In cases of harassment (this covers anything that interferes with peace or comfort). This requires evidence of the act and intent.

Conspiracy and Protection of Property Act 1875
In cases of false imprisonment (e.g. where someone is cornered against a wall, not allowed to leave a lift or their home).

Malicious Communications Act 1987
Where for example malicious letters are sent in the post likely to cause distress.

　　If you are considering taking legal action yourself, seek advice from a Law Centre or Citizens Advice Bureau. You may be able to get Legal Aid.

A secure environment

There is now much information available on improving security through design to minimise crime, generally giving residents greater security. These are some of the key principles to follow:
- ensuring that public spaces are overlooked by surrounding houses
- adequate fencing of private spaces, but designed so as not to create hiding spaces
- no ambiguity over what is private territory and what is public

- avoidance of alleys hidden from public gaze
- adequate lighting.[55]

A security package

An example of a good security package is one designed by Birmingham City Council 'to deter racial attacks and protect potential victims of racial harassment'. The 'standard basic pack' includes:

- personal alarms
- high security locks
- a still infra-red camera
- a sensitive tape recorder

In more serious cases additional equipment is issued to complete the pack. These packs include:

- infra red heat detection lights
- metal lockable letter boxes, fitted to the outside wall of the property
- fire resistant front doors and frames fitted with Chubb security locks and bolts
- opening window casements fitted with Chubb security locks and bolts.

They also have surveillance packs for more persistent or serious cases. These might include:

- infra red lamp

[55] London Research Centre *The National Directory of Action Against Racial Harassment* (1996), Lemos & Crane, covers the complete range of security measures used by social landlords.

- low light camera
- cabling
- monitor
- video recorder.[56]

Specialist staff

Landlords, particularly local authorities, have for a long time employed specialist staff to deal with cases of racial harassment, both to support the people experiencing harassment and to take action against the perpetrators. This has sometimes been criticised on the grounds that the result is that mainstream staff, both in the police and in housing departments for example, simply pass the case on to the specialist and do not take responsibility for dealing with it themselves. As it is unlikely ever to be the case that specialist staff will be able to deal with all the cases that might occur, this abdication of responsibility is likely to leave many cases unattended to and is also not going to build a body of knowledge and expertise within the organisation to deal with future attacks across a broad range of staff.

There is nonetheless a case for specialist staff. Some of the issues that arise out of racial harassment do need particular expertise, for example the issues around taking legal action and some of the issues around empathising with those experiencing racial harassment.

[56] *Racial harassment policy and procedure* (1993), Birmingham City Council. *The National Directory of Action Against Racial Harassment* covers the full range of equipment being employed nation-wide.

Example

The London Borough of Hounslow has employed three part-time members of staff to work on three of their estates – Ivybridge, Highfields and Heston Farm. Their role is to counsel those who have been attacked, encourage people to report attacks, set up educational programmes on the estates with other community organisations (including talks and discussions), establish self-help groups on the estates for those experiencing racial harassment to support each other and to raise awareness about racial harassment among all tenants.

The specialist staff also work not only with those who have experienced harassment but also with those at risk from it. Suresh Grover, Chair of the Hounslow monitoring project, said about the scheme

> 'It is the first time a local authority and community group have formed a partnership to work with people suffering racial harassment and the first time workers will be able to give on the spot front line support in emergency and non emergency situations. It is a unique scheme because it places the victim at the centre, both as a sufferer and someone who can take control to change their circumstances.'[57]

This targeted help is designed to empower those who are experiencing racial harassment. It enables them to seek help not only from authorities, but also from other sufferers of attacks. They are then able to support themselves in devising local solutions. This is a most welcome initiative.

---

[57]This initiative was widely reported – in *Inside Housing* and other housing journals.

However, one danger with support strategies for those experiencing racial harassment is that they unintentionally enforce the status of the person experiencing the harassment as a victim, disempowering them in ways that are discussed in previous chapters.

Self-help groups

A possible source of support for people who have suffered harassment is a self-help network of other people who have experienced harassment, either currently or in the past. It is an area of work that is now being developed.

> *Example*
> On the Silwood council estate in Lewisham there was a history of racial harassment – with racist graffiti, children being threatened with knives and physical assaults. In 1993, over a dozen of the families affected started to meet regularly with back-up from the local Race Equality Council. They provided mutual support and planned a campaign to force the council to take action. Council meetings were disrupted and discussions held with the Chair of the Housing Committee. These families were in fact rehoused, while criminal and civil proceedings have now started against the perpetrators on the estate. The families involved greatly benefited from sharing experiences, reducing the sense of isolation and powerlessness associated with the sense of facing problems alone, and gaining mutual emotional and practical support.[58]

[58] Reported in *Housing* magazine. The details were kindly supplied by Lewisham Racial Equality Council.

Emergency helplines

One of the more intractable aspects of racial harassment is
that the perpetrators do not confine their activities to
office hours. Whilst the police are available at all times, in
reality incidents of racial harassment may occur when the
police are at their most busy, for example when pubs close.
This means that, often, people experiencing harassment
are left entirely unsupported when they are most vulnerable, as the attack is taking place. In response some local
authorities have now established emergency 24-hour
helplines. This approach, although now pursued by many
authorities, was pioneered by Leicester City Council.

Example
Leicester City Council operates a dispersed alarm and
mobile warden service to over 6,000 clients, mostly
elderly people living in sheltered accommodation or
grouped housing schemes.

In 1989 the housing department decided to make
available alarms linked to the dispersed scheme to people
who had experienced, or were at risk of, racial harassment. Anyone who has experienced racial harassment
can be provided with a dispersed alarm unit following a
report of an incident. The scheme, however, is primarily
aimed at tenants on council estates.

The cost of unit provision and, where necessary, asso-
ciated works is borne by the authority. When the scheme
was established in 1989 the Council created an emergency support team of local authority staff volunteers,
mostly from the housing department. One volunteer team

leader was on call 24 hours a day to help co-ordinate the response. Many volunteers were from ethnic minority communities and had knowledge of minority languages.

Where an incident had been notified to the service control centre team, if the incident was going on at that moment – the control operator would immediately contact the police via a 999 call. This, together with the use of a unique client reference number, ensured an immediate police response. The control operator would also alert the duty team leader who would be responsible for deciding whether a response was required from the emergency support team. They also decided the appropriate mix of staff for the team and for liaison with the police.

The emergency support team had a broader remit than simply to stop an act of racial harassment. It also sought to initiate other remedies, such as emergency property repairs, removal of graffiti, contacting friends, provision of temporary accommodation and so on.

Written reports were made of incidents with copies going to relevant officers in the housing department, and to the City Council's legal section.

Up to the end of 1993, over 100 households had, at some point, a dispersed alarm unit installed. In December 1993 approximately 50 households had units linked to the control centre. Some of those installations are temporary, but they are only removed with the full agreement of the household if it feels that there is little likelihood of further racial harassment.

Between the beginning of 1990 and July 1993 there had been 116 calls concerned with racial harassment, of which 79 had involved attendance of the emergency support team.

The scheme has been successful in a number of ways: it provides additional reassurance to people in fear of further harassment. The swift response is also instrumental in stopping the escalation or repetition of incidents. The visibility of such incidents may also have acted as a disincentive to other potential aggressors. Also, court actions have been pursued through possession proceedings and injunctions. A few tenants threatened with court action have absconded.

Questions were raised at the end of 1993 about whether a 24-hour specialist standby team was necessary. This approach has been superseded by out-of-hours calls being dealt with directly by the police. Cases can be followed up by housing management staff on the next working day. This new approach does not appear to have undermined the scheme's effectiveness.

One potential danger with establishing specialist teams is that other parts of the organisation take the issue less seriously, simply referring it on. In fact, in Leicester's case, the idea of the response team had been furthered by a team-working approach in which the necessary skills and knowledge are vested in all staff.

Leicester City Council feels that the scheme represents 'a small but important element in the authority's strategy to combat racism.'[59]

---

[59] Reported in *Housing* magazine.

Advocacy

There are now many advocacy and community support projects for people experiencing racial harassment. They have improved reporting, providing support and assisting in getting evidence, as well as lobbying the police and local authorities to be more proactive in dealing with the problem of racial attacks and harassment.

One of the first to be formed was the Newham Monitoring Project, and its approach is illustrative of the role played by such community advocacy projects.

The Newham Monitoring Project was formed in 1980 in part as a result of Aktar Ali Baig's murder by four teenage skinheads for a £5 bet. They have subsequently campaigned for and developed an emergency and advice service for people experiencing racial harassment.

Example
Newham Monitoring Project told the journal *Legal Action* what happens when someone who is being racially harassed telephones:

'Take a pretty ordinary case of racial harassment. Somebody phones up the service and says they have been attacked. They have phoned the police and the police haven't come because there are people outside their house. The person answering their phone contacts a second volunteer who goes straight down there and supports the family in a practical way. Obviously, one thing is to keep pressing the police to come to the scene of the crime and arrest the perpetrators, if they are still around, or begin to try and identify them. Even today that doesn't

always happen. Then the person tells the family what we
can do and listens to what they want us to do. We try and
work in a non-patron/client way, instead building strategies together with those families. Sometimes there is
tremendous fear, they just can't take it anymore and are
desperate to get moved. We will take that up with the
Council the next day. In other cases they are determined
not to be driven out.

We follow the initial visit with regular liaison with the
family, involving them as much as they wish in their own
campaign. It's empowerment. We don't want people to
become dependent on us, but to be able to sort things out
for themselves as well.

Of course, each family has had its own experiences.
There are many different levels of anger and fear
involved. You have just got to be sensitive to that and try
to work out the best formula for action. There's no blue-
print. We tell all caseworkers, you learn on the ground.[60]

Working with other agencies

Apart from advocacy and community agencies, there may
also be other agencies whose support could be offered, like
victim support, local religious organisations, schools and
the education authorities, in assisting with transport for
the children to school and assisting the police for example.

Information about these other options should be given
as positive supplements to the landlord's action, not as
substitutes for supine inactivity on the landlord's part.

[60] *Legal Action*. The work of the Newham Monitoring Project is written up in the London
Research Centre, *National Directory of Action Against Racial Harassment* (1996), Lemos
& Crane. At the time of writing the Project's funding has been withdrawn by Newham
Council and its future is in doubt.

Getting the police involved

People who have been attacked may be ambivalent about the role of the police for reasons already discussed. Nonetheless the police can play an important role in reassuring people, and in deterring potential attackers. If the person who has been attacked agrees to involve the police, then the housing manager should know how to contact the right police officer who specialises in racial incidents or community policing. It should not be left to the person who has been attacked simply to contact the local police station, phone 999 or contact CID.

Rehousing

Whether people who have been racially harassed should be rehoused elsewhere remains one of the most vexed questions. Few believe that people should be expected to stay in the same home and suffer the attacks, and most people believe that in extreme circumstances temporary or permanent rehousing should be an option. There are, however, a number of concerns:

1. If the person who has been attacked is moved, this could be presented as a victory for the perpetrators. If their motive was to remove black people from the area, then they may in part have succeeded. This may encourage them to harass other black or ethnic minority people who move onto the estate or into the area.
2. The person who has been attacked will have the upset

and upheaval of moving, uprooting their immediate family, and breaking other family and social networks, suffering, in a way, the punishment while the perpetrator goes scot free.

3. Perhaps the person who has been attacked does not want to move at all, and may be very attached to a home on which they have lavished time, money and attention. They may only say they want to move because they believe that the landlord can take no effective action to stop the harassment.

4. The length of time it often takes to secure a transfer makes people accept properties that are not really suitable, with the result that further problems ensue and they are not happy in the new home. This is particularly likely where people have been desperate to move and have grown tired of waiting.

5. There is very little evidence for this, but it is sometime claimed that people will complain of racial harassment to secure a transfer, either when it is not occurring at all, or when it is not as serious as they are suggesting. All the evidence indicates that, very far from people exaggerating the extent of harassment, they often do not report it at all, or under-state the scale and severity of it.

6. Once the person is moved, they will be reluctant to give evidence in any case against the perpetrators. This response is understandable, and it is clearly wrong to deny them a transfer on these grounds. It is not the job of social landlords to use their tenants as 'canon fodder'. Nonetheless, it is still important to stress to

tenants that the landlord does wish to take action against perpetrators, and they would very much value their co-operation, and will support them if they do give evidence.

Rehousing options

If rehousing is considered the only option, then care should be taken that the properties that are identified as possible temporary or permanent moves are suitable. Properties would be unsuitable in an area:

• where there has previously been harassment
• where people will be isolated without family support, schools, suitable shops or religious centres.

If, in the interests of speed and because the people who have been harassed are frightened and desperate, a less than suitable property is offered and accepted, it should be treated as a temporary move, with a view to a more suitable move being identified as soon as possible.

It is not always possible to give people an indication of exactly how long they will have to wait for a suitable property to be offered to them. Tenants, however, do often have unrealistic expectations about how quickly suitable properties for transfer can be identified. Whilst it would be inappropriate to use the length of the wait as a means of putting people off a transfer, it is also important to be honest about the average length of the wait, and what other options there are for action while a suitable property is being identified.

Seeking a transfer should not be seen as an alternative

to any of the other actions discussed in this chapter as ways of supporting people who have been attacked, or indeed the options for taking action against perpetrators discussed in chapter 7. People who have been attacked can then consider these factors, alongside their other concerns about the suitability of a property and its location, and decide whether or not they will accept the offer.

Reletting

There is also a dilemma about reletting the property that has been vacated by the people who experienced the harassment. It is iniquitous, not to mention illegal, to regard that property as a no-go area for black and ethnic minority people. The property should be allocated in the normal way; however, if the property is to be offered to a black or other ethnic minority person they should be told the history, the landlord's polices in combating harassment, and that if they turn the offer down they will be made another offer. They will be less likely to turn the offer down if the landlord can show that effective action has already been taken against those responsible for the harassment.

Financial assistance

Counsel's opinion was sought by the London Borough of Lewisham[61] on the question of financial assistance to 'victims of racist attacks who transfer as a consequence'. The advice the council was given was that payments directly

---

[61] London Borough of Lewisham Race Relations Committee (1988), *Financial assistance for council tenants who are victims of racist attacks and who transfer as a consequence.*

related to removal expenses can be made (under Section 26(1) of the Housing Act 1985). This could cover items such as:

• removal of household fittings and furniture
• disconnections and reconnections
• refixing a TV aerial
• change of address labels
• loss of wages
• adapting floor coverings and curtains
• professional fees.

This list is not exhaustive. In addition, Counsel advised that a possible form of compensation for distress, suffering and hardship would be sums paid for the distress caused by the harassment and the tenant having to leave the property in which they have lived for a number of years (pursuant to Section 71 of the Race Relations Act 1976) in the interests of improving race relations, provided that the council keeps an open mind about the figure and considers each case on its merits.

Other social landlords, such as housing associations, have rather greater latitude in the matter of financial support and compensation. There can however be little argument that the involuntary loss of one's home is a matter justly deserving compensation.

CHAPTER 9

FOLLOW-UP VISITS
Structure / Future visits if harassment persists

After an initial report of an incident of racial harassment it may very well be the case that incidents are followed up and action is taken either by the person who conducted the original interview, the housing manager, or by their line manager. One criticism made against social landlords is that they do not keep their tenants informed about the actions they are taking and they do not make follow-up visits to ensure that the tenants feel secure and that some action has resulted from the initial visit.

The consequence of this is that tenants often feel that not enough has been done, or worse still that nothing can be done. The impact of this is to create a vicious circle of tenants thinking: if nothing can be done then there is no point in reporting an incident. If an incident is not reported the consequence is undoubtedly that nothing is done. This self-fulfilling circle makes the problem of racial attacks and harassment significantly harder to deal with.

Follow-up visits are therefore essential to tenants to give them news of any action that has been taken and any other consequences that have arisen from the original incident. The other important function of follow-up visits is to see whether there has been any recurrence of the harassment or any further incidents since the first visit which have not been reported to the housing officer. There is much evidence to suggest that harassment, if unchallenged, is likely to recur. It does not always follow that tenants will report other incidents so the onus should be on housing managers to make follow-up visits, as a matter of course, to check whether or not there have been any further incidents.

The final reason for making follow-up visits is to again reassure the tenant about the commitment to their safety and well-being. Physical attendance at the property is more likely to do this than a letter or a telephone call.

Structure

The four main objectives of a follow-up visit are:
1. To make sure that the tenant is all right. The housing manager will want to know whether any further incidents have occurred. If so, they should gather information as for the initial visit.
2. To ask whether any further support is needed or can be provided. Again the housing officer should generate options with the tenant before asking them to make a choice about what they think would be appropriate. Discussion of options follows the pattern of the first interview.
3. To report back on any action that has already been

taken and any consequences that have followed. The importance of this cannot be overstated.

4. To agree any further action that will be taken and to make an arrangement for visiting again if there have been any further incidents.

Future visits if harassment persists

At each visit to the person who has been harassed the interviewer should emphasise the importance of being contacted again if there are any incidents. It is also good practice to keep in regular touch with people who have been harassed to ensure that no further incidents occur, regardless of whether or not they contact the housing manager.

If the harassment persists, then the housing manager will want to discuss in more detail:

- the support that can be provided
- gathering detailed evidence against perpetrators
- visiting as many witnesses as possible
- preparing for action against the perpetrators.

The interviewer needs to liaise early on with their legal representatives to get their advice on how to gather evidence for future action, ensure that the tenant is well briefed on collecting this evidence, and ensure that everyone else who might be witnesses (neighbours, caretakers, estate-based staff, maintenance staff) are briefed on the need to report all incidents.

A discussion on appropriate action will be needed now that warnings to the perpetrators appear to be failing.

- Is an injunction possible? What would be needed to get the injunction? Would it work? etc.
- Are the perpetrators tenants of the same landlord? Should notice of seeking possession be served? What might the consequences of that be? etc.
- What action could the police or other agencies take?

Rehousing also has to be discussed as a more real possibility if that is what the person being harassed wants, and the detailed procedures initiated to elicit an alternative property.

APPENDIX

A. SAMPLE CASE RECORDS

1. PREPARATION

Name of housing officer
Joan Benjamin

Name and address of person experiencing harassment
Joygun Bibi

What is known so far
Youths congregating at bottom of staircase stopping her from getting up to her flat and insulting her

How the harassment was reported
She called on the caretaker

Date of report
Monday 30 September 1996

Any emergency action already been taken
Caretaker dispersed group of youths and phoned neighbourhood office. I called in on Joygun Bibi when on another visit later in the afternoon to make arrangements for interview

Have all the arrangements for interview been made	
Agreed place	*41 Rothbury House, Mrs Bibi's home*
Agreed time and date	*Wednesday 2 October 11.30 a.m.*
Language for interview	*Bengali*
Name of interpreter if needed	*Saleha Khatun*
Any preference expressed for race or gender of interviewer	*No but wanted female interpreter*
Checklist of documents for interview	
Copy of full policy and procedure *Copy of summary of action landlord will take* *List of potential agencies which may be of help with names and phone numbers*	

2. MEETING

People present	
Name(s) of housing officer(s)	*Joan Benjamin*
Name of interpreter	*Saleha Khatun*
Person experiencing harassment	*Joygun Bibi*
Their advocate(s)	*Jahanara Begum (sister-in-law)*
Their address	*21 Myrtle Gardens NE6*
Date, time and place of meeting	
41 Rothbury House NE6. Wednesday 2 October. 11.30 a.m.	

Details of what has just happened
Joygun Bibi took the children to school and then went to the shops. She came back with 2 large bags. There were 4 boys – aged between 15 and 17 – sitting around at the bottom of her staircase. Her flat is on the second floor. There was no room for her to get past. She asked them to move, but they took no notice. She stood there for a little while and then asked again. Then they started shouting at her. She didn't understand much of what they said, but it was very aggressive indeed. She knows they said "fucking Paki" more than once. One boy kept jabbing his finger and another one took a kick at one of her bags of shopping. She had seen the caretaker sweeping up on her way back from the shops so she went to find him, still trying to carry all the shopping. She got him to come with her. The boys could see them coming back and went off in the other direction before they arrived. The caretaker called on the boys to stop but they didn't.

Details of where and when it happened
Bottom of staircase to 35–49 Rothbury House. Monday 25 November. About 10.15 a.m.

Details of people responsible
Two of the boys she has often seen on the estate before, and one of them she knows hangs around in the mini-cab office on Cavendish Way. The two she has often seen before are both tall. The first one is thin. Whenever she sees him he is always wearing the same blue anorak. He has light brown hair thick on top but shaved very short at the back and sides. The other one – seen at the mini cab office – has black hair and sometimes has a dog with him. He was wearing a grey sports sweatshirt. The other two boys she hasn't seen before and she couldn't give much of a description. They were both white.

Details of any witnesses
The Caretaker. Mrs Harris at No 35 is elderly and usually at home. She might have heard what was going on.

Details of how it has affected the household being interviewed
Joygun Bibi is a widow with three children at school. She's been very nervous to go out since the incident and her sister-in-law Jahanara Begum has had to come round to help take the children to school. Jahanara's own children are at another school, and because of this she hasn't been able to get them there on time yesterday or today.

Details of any previous history of harassment
The two boys Joygun Bibi has often seen on the estate have shouted at her and the children before – she is definite about two previous occasions. She's just walked by taking no notice, pretending she hasn't heard.

Date time and place of next meeting
Monday 7 October 11 a.m.

B. PLAN OF ACTION

What action has been agreed	Who is taking the action	By when	Who else should be contacted

Support from landlord

Keep an eye out for return of youths, and try to talk to them	*Caretaker*	*This p.m.*	*Relief Caretaker*
Collect mobile phone from office, leave emergency numbers to call if they come back	*Joan Benjamin*	*This p.m.*	*Team leader*
Talk to Sally Adebayo at residents association	*Joan Benjamin*	*Friday p.m.*	

Action against perpetrators by landlord

Talk to caretaker about possible identification, previous incidents and any info on mini-cab office	*Joan Benjamin*	*This p.m.*	
Talk to Mrs Harris to see if she knows anything	*Joan Benjamin*	*Friday p.m.*	
If anyone identified – report back to Joygun Bibi before deciding further steps	*Joan Benjamin*	*Next meeting*	

What action has been agreed	Who is taking the action	By when	Who else should be contacted

Action by person reporting harassment

Contact Bangladesh Welfare Association	*Jahanara Begum*	*Thursday*	
Won't use diary sheets, but will record any further incidents on tape (can use son's tape machine). They can be translated	*Joygun Bibi*	*As and when*	*Saleha Khatun*

Involvement of other agencies

Bangladesh Welfare Association – visit and possibly get someone round for a few days at times when Joygun Bibi is going out?	*Ataur Rahman?*	*Next meeting*	
Residents association – tell of incident. Check if Sally thinks there's a connection with nuisance problems discussed at last officers' meeting with the association	*Sally Adebayo*	*Friday p.m.*	*Team leader*
Multi-agency working group – report case and see if they have any suggestions	*David Headlam*	*Friday p.m.*	

C. Tenant's Diary Record

Please describe what has just happened

Write down where and when it happened (include the exact time and date if you can)

What details have you got of people responsible (if you don't know their name, describe what they looked like, or where you think they live, or the names of other people you think they are friendly with)

What details are there of anyone else who saw what happened? (if you know how to get in touch with them, write that down too):

How has this affected you (and your family)?

Who else have you told about this?

INDEX

Lemos & Crane publishes books for people seeking essential, accessible and high quality information and ideas written by leading experts and practitioners on racial harassment, housing law and practice, business and management – including education management – and social change.

Lemos & Crane authors and series editors include Andrew Arden QC, Charles Handy, Mike Pedler, Peter Townsend and Michael Young.

Lemos & Crane books are available through good bookshops. Your bookseller can order any Lemos & Crane book for you and have it available within a few days.

Information about all titles available from:
Lemos & Crane
20 Pond Square
Highgate Village
London N6 6BA
Tel: 0181-348 8263
Fax: 0181-347 5740
Email: sales@lemos.demon.co.uk

Dealing with racial harassment

"One of the most dispiriting aspects of race relations in this country" was the way that Kenneth Clarke described racial harassment. Lemos & Crane are at the leading edge of developing good practice. Our work in this area is second to none.

National Directory of Action Against Racial Harassment
London Research Centre

"It is rare to be able to recommend a book that could make a real difference to people's lives but the *National Directory of Action Against Racial Harassment* provides us with a great opportunity to do just that. This is an invaluable guide to good practice and multi-agency work and a vital source for everybody dealing with these crimes – from victims and advice workers to police officers, council workers and teachers."
Sir Herman Ouseley, Chair of the Commission for Racial Equality

"What is exciting about the Directory is that it shows for the first time in one place what is happening up and down the country and how different agencies are working together. It is about good practice and everybody will learn from it."
Helena Kennedy QC

Broken down into sub-regions, from the South West of England to the Highlands of Scotland, the National Directory identifies hundreds of initiatives and agencies who can support people under attack and pursue those responsible. It also highlights working on prevention and makes clear that in many cases prevention is possible.

Paperback   592pp   234 x 156mm   ISBN 1-898001-27-8

Eliminating Racial Harassment
Richard Seager and Joanna Jeffery

"This book could form part of a required list for all involved in this vital area of housing management." *Housing*

"Anyone working to encourage good practice among housing providers will find this a useful publication." *The Adviser*

"...the guidance in this book provides an important framework for the development of successful strategies to help eliminate racial harassment." Sir Herman Ouseley, Chair of the Commission for Racial Equality

A comprehensive, clear and concise manual on practical policies and procedures to tackle racial harassment, this book will ensure that housing organisations not only have policies, but also that they are effective.

Paperback   132pp   216 x 138mm   ISBN 1-898001-01-4

Interviewing Perpetrators of Racial Harassment
Gerard Lemos

"No area office should be without a copy." *Housing*

"The book is highly recommended." *HARUNews*

Endorsed by the Chartered Institute of Housing and the Housing Corporation, this is the first handbook for housing managers in local authorities and housing associations giving practical guidance on how to interview perpetrators and stop racial harassment before legal action is necessary.

Paperback   96pp   216 x 138mm   ISBN 1-898001-00-6

Training video

Allegations and Action
a training video on effective interviewing skills for dealing with racial harassment in housing
Lemos & Crane
sponsored by the Housing Corporation

To stop racial harassment, prompt and complete information from those attacked and effective action against perpetrators is essential. Yet housing officers may be uncertain or even frightened about talking to those against whom allegations are made. For the first time, here is an authoritative training video which explores how it should be done.

The video consists of three dramatised case studies – based on researching real cases. These make compelling drama in themselves, as well as being triggers for discussion and learning. In addition the video contains interviews with practising housing managers, providing a powerful insight into real life problems. The video is not a campaigning tool, nor a documentary. Its purpose is learning. The issues are complex and the video will be invaluable in developing effective action to deal with allegations of racial harassment and support for people experiencing it.

A training booklet with comprehensive notes is provided to ensure that viewers derive the maximum benefit. The notes explore the context for racial harassment in housing, as well as drawing out the key learning points for group leaders and participants to draw from using the materials. The video and notes allow managers to provide cost effective timely training for staff dealing with this pressing and sometimes intractable problem.

30 minute video cassette and training materials.
Available from May 1997
Please send for full Information leaflet to Lemos & Crane.